PEOPLE IN PIECES II

MILDER VERSIONS OF MULTIPLE
PERSONALITY DISORDER

**IF YOU ARE INTRIGUED BY THE PAINTING BELOW,
YOU MIGHT CONSIDER READING THE BOOK.**

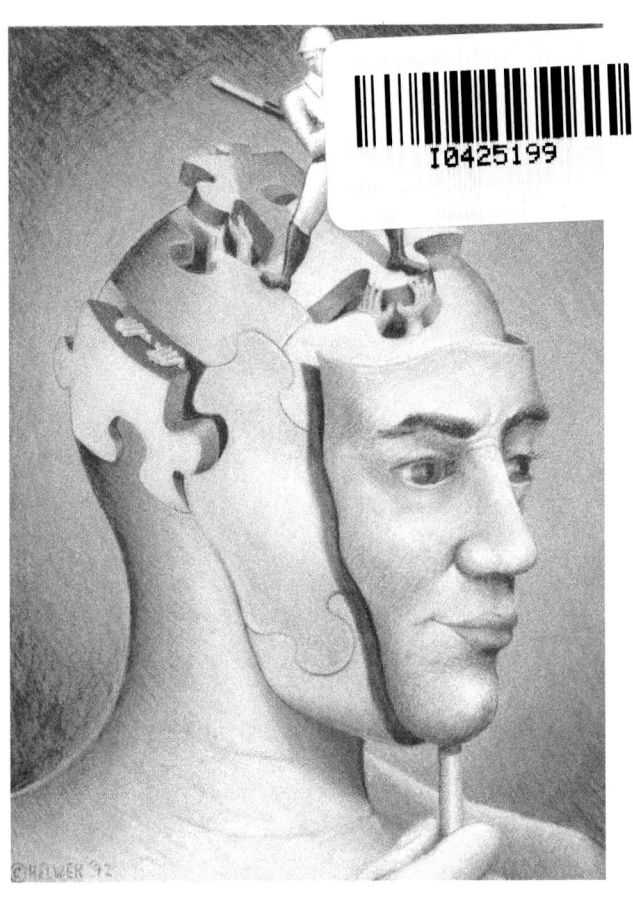

ALAN MARSHALL, PH.D.

ISBN:1-4609-1608-5
ISBN-13:978-1-4609-1608-7
LCCN: 2011902331

Dedication

First of all, I want to thank my patients from over the last 4 decades of my practice. They have been exceedingly "patient" with me, and have taught me most of whatever it is I know.

But mostly I want to thank my family - my wife Gail and my two sons - Chris and Joel. They have stuck with me through some very dark times, and I appreciate that more than I can ever say. I love you very much.

Foreword (1993)

Jacques Cousteau was a lucky man. He explored depths of the sea where he witnessed a very different and fascinating world from the ordinary. Psychotherapists are lucky also. The world in which they work is quite different from the usual workaday world. They are permitted access to a realm of human experience that lies beyond the routine. They are invited to accompany people into the domain of the Unconscious, and are paid to be guides in that strange and sometimes forbidding territory.

For both Cousteau and psychotherapists, there is an implied responsibility. If in their explorations they stumble upon something noteworthy, they are expected to report it, with as much candor and accuracy as possible. Even if the subject matter is not entirely new, they may witness it at a different depth or from another perspective. And when seen in that way, it may prove helpful or enlightening in some regard.

That's how this book came into being. I've been engaged and fascinated by the subject for over two decades. The written account of my experiences is what scientists call a Hypothetical Model. A Model does not claim to be "The Truth." Rather it is one way of looking at the phenomena that hopefully provides for some degree of elucidation, and suggests paths for further inquiry. To whatever extent the Model fits with and sheds light on the subject, it is of value. I have no doubt that it will in its turn be replaced by something more illuminating. If the present work provides a means to that improvement, it will be worth it.

Foreword (2011)

It has been 18 years since this book was first published. Over the years, I've realized that a number of things I said were incomplete, or in some cases, simply wrong. That's why there is a new edition. Most of it is the same, except for the second and third chapters, which are almost entirely new.

The comment about the painting on the front of this book is meant to be taken seriously. If it strikes a chord in you, you might want to read the book. The obverse is also true, however: if it does NOT strike a chord, the book will probably be a waste of time for you. I believe that people who have never separated into Ego States, or dissociated, have no way to understand the phenomenon, no matter how hard they try. I don't want them to be frustrated.

The book does focus on a kind of dysfunction called Ego State Disorder and the underlying process called "dissociation." Some people who are experiencing intolerable levels of physical or emotional pain automatically go into a mental state very much like "shock." They become unaware of the pain, and their brain transports them to a different mental place, where the pain does not exist. Once the pain abates to a manageable level, they return to normal consciousness. There will still be substantial pain to deal with, but it will not be such as to require that they exit their bodies.

The process is analogous to what happens when an electrical circuit is overloaded: the fuse or circuit breaker trips, the current is interrupted, and the circuit is protected. However, just as is true in psychological and physical shock, the underlying problem that required the disconnection has not yet been addressed. One of the most amazing things about dissociation is that, even though the person stops feeling the pain temporarily, the memory of it is preserved forever in the brain. (Let's leave False Memory Syndrome alone for the present.) I can only speculate about why the human species would want to preserve such memories. But I believe the answer has something to do with healing. It seems as though the brain stores traumatic memories because it can be very important to the person to remember them at some point in the future. I realize that this is purely a guess, but I have seen too many instances of it in action to discount it entirely. The retrieval of some kinds of terrible memories has the ability to restore sanity and a sense of wholeness that have been lost, once they are regained. It's kind of like the photograph: some people will understand all this, and sense that it is vital for them to retrieve those memories. Other people will think it is silly and a waste of time. If you're one of those, you should probably put the book back on the shelf. If you're one of the others, welcome.

Chapter I
"Sally"

Sally's daddy is screaming at her. He does it a lot. She can never seem to figure out what it was she did that was so bad. The shouting is hurting her head and the tears are burning her eyes and she wants to run away. But she can't. He's bigger and faster and would catch her and make it a lot worse. Just when she can't endure another moment of this, a magical thing happens: she leaves her body. Not physically, but mentally. Her body is still there just like before, but now there is a vacant look in her eyes. Because her mind has taken her to another place. Just when her little heart was about to break, her brain tripped a switch, and she found herself in her grandma's lap eating freshly-baked brownies. She stays there until she gets a signal that it is safe to return home.

What happened is that Sally "dissociated." She did not *cause* it to happen, it was completely automatic. As I said above, it's like what happens when a person

1

is badly wounded, or close to death: they sometimes go into "shock." They are still awake, but they are not really aware of what is happening in the present. The brain does this instinctively when the pain level gets too severe to be consciously tolerated.

I want to propose three different ways that this story could develop. First, it could turn out okay, in which case Sally would rarely have to experience this sort of thing, and would grow up to be a normal adult. Second, things could get much worse: she could experience this frequently, along with other kinds of serious abuse, and grow up to have a Multiple Personality Disorder. Or third, it could turn out somewhere in between, in which case she might develop what I'll call an "Ego State Disorder", which is what this book is about. This disorder does not currently exist as a named item in the official Diagnostic and Statistical Manual. It, and Multiple Personality Disorder, fall under another general category called "Dissociative Identity Disorder."

I don't think the name change has added any clarity to the problems, and will continue to use the old term, along with the new one, "Ego State Disorder". The latter term was, to my knowledge, first coined by

Dr. John and Helen Watkins, who did some of the earliest work on it.

I'll describe Ego State Disorder by contrasting it with the other conditions - normalcy and Multiple Personality. If you were to see it on a graph, it would look like this:

DEGREES OF DISSOCIATION

Minimal	Mild	Severe
Normal	ESD	MPD

Note that the line describes a *continuum* of degrees of dissociation. A particular person might fall anywhere along the line. A person can have a very mild case of ESD, so that he would fall between "normal" and "ESD." or a mild case of MPD, and fall between ESD and MPD.

NORMAL SALLY

Let's say her dad only screams at her occasionally, and her life is generally pretty good. Her mom loves her, almost as much as her grandma, and her dad is just moody. She'll probably be fine. Sure, there will be times when things will get real bad, and her brain might on those rare occasions have to trip that switch again. But not very often. And it might even come in handy sometimes. If she has to sit in a dentist's chair for hours on end having a painful root canal, she might be glad to have this capacity to "go somewhere else" in her mind, and leave her body, at least temporarily.

Normal Sally may not be exactly the same person all the time. She will certainly behave differently at a raucous birthday party than at a church social. And she might be quite moody, like her father. Sometimes she might care for him deeply, and at other times despise him (say, during adolescence!). But basically she will be one person nearly all the time despite the variability in moods and attitudes. She will have a simple, uncomplicated sense of who she is and what she does and does not like. And she will probably remember a few key events from almost every year of her life after age three or four.

SALLY AS A MULTIPLE PERSONALITY

Now to the opposite end of the continuum - to Multiple Personality. To get here, Sally's life will have to be much worse. There will be a great likelihood that the abuse she is subjected to will be not only emotional, but also sexual as well. The abuse will occur often, usually at the hands of a trusted adult.

(Molestation by a sibling or another youngster is not usually as traumatic unless it involves great physical pain.) It is possible that there will be someone in her life who will love her, but even that will be tainted by the fact that this person is unable or unwilling to protect her from the horror of the abuse. Each time the abuse occurs, her brain will throw the exit switch and she will enter the world of fantasy.

Imagine, if you will, what happens to her then. After the adult is finished with her (I know how crude that sounds, but it is how part of the child feels it), she has to eventually come back to reality. What is she supposed to do then? She has no idea where she has been for the last period of time, or how she got back into the present. Circumstances have changed, but why did she not know when they did? How did she get her clothes so messed up? Where did the blood come from? All these things can quickly lead to thoughts like "I must be crazy!" or "I must have done something really bad." or "I'm just a bad person."

She probably has a vague awareness that she is forbidden to tell anyone how confused she feels, or how rotten. This conviction would have been implanted during the abuse by the adult, so that she can only vaguely remember it. The abuser would perhaps have told her that no one would believe her anyway, and that if she told her mother, it would kill her. Or some such. The content varies, but the effect is always the same: muteness and secrecy for the child. But deep inside her, she feels an urge to kill someone, quite possibly herself. Ten different emotions and voices rage inside her simultaneously. How can she be expected to make any sense of all that? Simply put, she cannot. And so she spends much of her life in a daze, unable to concentrate at school or anywhere else. She doesn't look like the Sally we knew before. Her smile is waxy and half-hearted, and her movements are stiff. But she manages to put one foot in front of the other, and to do the best she can. For now, she gets to the bathroom and scrubs herself everywhere she can reach. After a while, she feels a little better. She puts on some clean clothes and goes outside to pretend to play.

Now, assuming again that this kind of trauma is repeated fairly often, a very fundamental change begins to take place in Sally's brain. She starts to develop a distinct and separate portion of her personality we call an Alter. Sally is a little girl, and little children love their parents even when they are treated extremely poorly by them. They will find all sorts of excuses for their parents' abusive behavior, so that they can preserve their love for them, and the hope that they will be loved BY them. Usually this takes a form something like "It's all my fault. If I could just do what they say and keep my mouth shut." This sort of thinking signals the beginning of self-loathing and self-distrust. Just one portion of the terrible legacy of child abuse.

But what if they don't stop abusing her? What if she behaves perfectly and keeps her mouth shut, and they continue the same horrors? Little by little, a part of Sally's brain begins to realize the truth - that it's not stopping and shows no evidence of doing so. That part becomes furious with the parents, and tries to force Sally to fight back, or to tell someone what is happening, or to at least face the truth herself. But she cannot, and she knows it. She cannot even allow herself to *think* those kinds of thoughts, and refuses to listen to the part of herself that knows the truth

Once this conflict escalates sufficiently, the forbidden thoughts and feelings have to go into hiding. They are now beginning to coalesce into a split-off part we've called an Alter. It will continue to haunt Sally, mostly in places like her nightmares, which will become very frequent. There might also be times when it sneaks out, for example, during competitive sports. Sally might really hurt somebody toward whom she feels no conscious anger, just because that forbidden part HAS to get out some anger somewhere, sometime. She is eaten up with it, and cannot contain it perfectly. It's too powerful.

Because it's so powerful, it is a great deal of work for Sally to keep it corralled. It takes a lot of her energy to do it. She will probably seem lethargic to her teachers, and easily discouraged. She won't seem to have the energy that most other children have, or as much curiosity or enthusiasm about things in general.

This is an example of how the first Alter might be created. But in true Multiple Personality Disorder there may be many more than one. Large numbers of Alters have been reported, but all are formed from the same basic recipe: unresolvable conflict. One person cannot simultaneously feel two or more emotions at the same time if they are dramatically different. You may at times love and hate the same person, but you experience those feelings at different times. When a child feels all the natural love for his/her parents that is there instinctively, and is as well totally dependent on them, and yet is frequently treated horribly by them, something has to give. The brain has to split. When it does, an Alter is formed. Once a part of the brain becomes dedicated to preserving terrible feelings that cannot be consciously felt, and thoughts that cannot be thought, the remaining parts of the brain are depleted. It is no longer operating as one whole system. It becomes fragmented, and the various fragments become severely antagonistic toward each other.

If you feel up to it, try to put yourself inside the brain of a child who is in the process of being sexually abused. First, the abuser is probably a trusted adult, and the process may begin very benignly, with offers of candy, affection, or some other attraction. The child at first feels special to be getting this attention, and grateful for it. Soon, there will be physical "play" which the child once again may enjoy, as long as it is not painful. But that only lasts so long. As the adult becomes more aroused, he becomes more centered on his own pleasure, and much less interested in the child's experience. Finally, there is total self-absorption, usually great physical pain to the child, and a terrible feeling of betrayal by this "trusted" adult. Depending on the child's age, there are usually threats to never tell anyone, which are delivered with such energy and conviction that the child does just as she is told.

Now consider what is going on inside the child's head during all this. First, there are thoughts of "He loves me. He's taking special time with me" etc. Then there is often the physical pleasure which the body has no way to resist, as long as it is painless. Thoughts are like "This feels good. He really does love me." And then when it turns painful, "What happened?! Doesn't he see that I'm crying? Why does he want to hurt me?" And thoughts of the betrayal like "I thought he loved me. How can he do this to me? Did I do something terribly wrong to deserve this?" And afterward, "I don't understand! How could he do this? I'll never trust him again. I hate him!!" And finally, "But I know I can never tell anyone. He's right - nobody would ever believe me, and I'm too ashamed to tell anyway."

What we see here are wide ranges of emotional and thought responses in the same person. Within a short period of time, the child has loved and loathed the adult, has totally trusted and totally distrusted him, and felt physical pleasure and great physical pain from him. The confusion and conflict is disabling. No child's brain can handle it.

Assuming that the adult figures out ways to continue the molestation (which they almost always do), the conflict only intensifies. One part of the child insists that it's her own fault, and that she just needs to be more obedient for things to go back to the way they were before the abuse. The Bible, and society, say to "respect your elders", and all the adults around her might think that the abuser is a good, upstanding Christian man. So it must be all her fault. (And one of the appealing things about that thought is that it makes the situation appear to be *fixable*. All she has to do is be a good girl and she can continue to believe that it will all go away.)

The opposing, negative thoughts have no such promise built into them. They foretell doom, more of the same misery, with no shred of hope for things to be better. The man is a bastard, is cruel and totally selfish, and will never change.

But what child would want to think any such thing? Sally certainly does not, and screams at the other part of herself to "Quit saying those ugly things to me! Shut up! Go away forever!!"

They don't go away, but they do become more subdued. That part of her brain knows that she hates it, and never wants to hear from it again. So it recedes into the background, always looking for opportunities when Sally is not in complete control to exert itself, to express what it knows to be the truth, which it comes to value more than life itself.

The point of all this, for present purposes, is to describe how and why the brain splits itself into various parts, because of their irreconcilable differences. Now let's see how this same basic process occurs in milder forms, in Ego State Disorders.

SALLY WITH EGO STATE DISORDER

This is the middle ground between normalcy and Multiplicity. In this case, Sally might still be sexually abused, but less often, and more likely by someone she did not know or trust. He would still make sure she did not tell, and it would still be very traumatic, but not as bad as it would if it were a parent or a loved one. And the abuse wouldn't have to be of a sexual nature. It could be humiliation or physical beating.

But overall, there would be more love and nurturing in her life than in the case of Multiplicity. There would not be as many periods of her life that she could not remember, but still she would notice that there was a big difference between her amount of recall and that of her friends.

She would very likely be indecisive, often because of not knowing how she really felt about something. It would bother her that she would be more change-able than most people. Her friends might find her fickle and untrustworthy. In general, she would find that she *had* fewer feelings than most people - at least ones that she could identify. There would always be a gnawing sense of incompleteness, and only a dim awareness of what it might be like to be whole.

Like a Multiple, she would have some number of different personality Parts, but they would not have the individuality or solidity or separateness of Alters. They would not have the power to completely take over her behavior, and they would not cause her the same amount of conflict and confusion as occurs with Alters.

She might live out her entire life this way, only vaguely aware of her deficits. She might well be able to hold a decent job, although it would take a lot more out of her than most people. There would be relatively few things she would really enjoy, and she would have no idea why that was.

There would be symptoms, though. Always. She might have panic attacks, or migraine headaches, or addictions, or any other symptom imaginable. During periods when she was not in good control, the Parts would exert themselves, taking advantage of her temporary weakness to assert themselves. (Remember the painting on the front of the book? That's "them" - the Parts - trying to get out into consciousness.) She would then do things which seemed "out of character for her", things orchestrated by the Parts still trying to get her to see the truths that they know about, which she has repressed.

Sometimes a woman with ESD will be triggered when her daughter gets to the same age as she was when the abuse occurred. At such times a particular look in the child's eye, or some little gesture, might catapult her back into her own childhood, quite out of control. And for the thousandth time the thought would be there: "What's wrong with me? What IS it?"

SUMMARY OF MPD - ESD DIFFERENCES:

1. MPD usually involves a number of Alters ranging from 3 to 15. ESD Parts more often number in the 2 to 5 range.

2. Alters can surface completely on their own, and take over behavior and attitudes completely. The adult usually has amnesia for that period of time. Parts usually have to be elicited, or invited, to come out. They rarely speak in their own voice (nor do they necessarily *have* one). They rarely take over the person's behavior completely. They are more likely to assert themselves and their point of view in day- or night dreams.

3. Alters almost always are at war with each other, or at least some of the others. The conflicts are so intense that one Alter may talk about wanting, or trying, to kill others (or the adult person, which happens frequently). The conflicts among Parts are rarely that intense, and are more often centered around one Part trying to prevent another from talking, or revealing its memories.

4. When a shift occurs in MPD from the adult to an Alter or from one Alter to another, there is almost

always a violent physical response. There may be an intense, brief headache, or bodily shaking, or some such response. This gives some idea of the intensity of the electrical changes in the brain during the shift. There is almost never any similar physical response of Parts in ESD during shifting. It is much more subtle, and the electrical activity in the brain is apparently not nearly as powerful.

5. In MPD, when an Alter takes control, the adult often has no idea what occurs from that point on. The Alter can take total control of the body without any awareness on the part of the adult. In extreme cases, this means that one Alter can literally commit murder without involving the adult at all. When Kenneth Bianchi (the Los Angeles "hillside strangler") was arrested, he had no idea why. He was dumbfounded, and he wasn't kidding. He had no - zero - awareness of having done anyone any harm. All he knew was that he blacked out from time to time. It was not until he consented to hypnosis with Dr. John Watkins that it became apparent that there was someone else in there, someone who had in fact killed people.

DR. WATKINS (1984) WRITES:

"I found Kenneth Bianchi to b a pleasant, mild young man who seemed to be earnestly seeking to understand what had happened and why he was in jail charged with two murders. In describing his child-hood, he stated that he had always thought well of his mother. ('I would have fought anyone who said anything against her.'), but that he had recently been shown medical records which brought many doubts to his mind. Reports of his many visits to physicians, school counselors, social workers, and examining psy-chologists portrayed his mother as having been dom-inating, over-concerned, trotting him from one clinic to another for his 'nervous' problems (petit mal, aller-gies, tic, incontinence, many phobias), and refusing to accept psychiatric opinions of an emotional basis for his symptoms. She was also reported to have been both seductive (showing him nude pictures) and cruel (punishing him by holding his hand over a stove burner and beating him with a belt)."

After a number of hypnotic sessions, Kenneth began to have very painful headaches. These proved to be harbingers of the emergence of "Steve", the Alter who did the killing. Finally, Dr. Watkins encouraged

Kenneth to try to focus on the headaches and see if he could discern what was causing them. That was when the Alter "Steve" burst forth.

Steve was furious with Dr. Watkins for exposing him. While he remained safely in the background, Steve could do whatever he wanted and not be held accountable. But once his existence was discovered, he would also become known to Kenneth. And that meant trouble. First, because Kenneth would then have to admit to being at least an accessory to the murders. But more importantly to Steve, he would become severely limited in carrying out his psycho-pathic behaviors once Kenneth knew to watch out for him. Even though Steve hated Dr. Watkins, he was delighted to finally have the opportunity to brag about the murders. He eagerly pointed out the pic-tures in an L.A. paper of which girls he had killed and which ones were killed by his cousin, Angelo Buono."

Unfortunately, the phenomenon is all too real. There is more and more experimental evidence to support the highly diverse nature of the Alters. For example, each Alter responds quite differently to EEG's (Pitblado, 1986). There is also evidence that different Alters repond very differently to medications! Some are far-sighted and some are near-sighted. Some are allergic to poison ivy and some are not. The list of differences is endless.

With ESD Parts, it is quite different. I have never known of a case where the adult person was totally unaware of what one or more of the Parts were doing. They might not like it, and might not be able to stop it, but they always knew what was happening. There was no true amnesia.

SUMMARY OF MPD - ESD SIMILARITIES:

1. Both seem to almost always involve memories of trauma. These memories always involve truths that the adult cannot bear to think about. Alters and Parts both know that what they remember is (at least from their perspective) the truth, and will not surrender it, period. It's really a wonderful commitment to a valuable principle, but has its drawbacks, as we'll see later.

2. Both seem to get "locked" in time, right around the point of their development. They are not able to mature as a normal person would, and persist in their feelings and points of view almost exactly as they were at the point of inception. They find it

almost impossible to change, and resist "outside information" at all cost. They know what they know, and do not want to be influenced by others in any way. This stymies their development, and makes for slower movement in therapy. But trying to force them in any way to speed up only leads to disaster.

3. At the same time, paradoxically, both *can be* vital sources of information in therapy. IF their trust can be gained (understandably a lengthy process), they can provide a nearly complete history of the person's development, and especially of the painful events that are repressed and forgotten. Thus they are the greatest enemies of, and at the same time potentially the greatest allies of, therapy.

With hopefully some understanding of the nature of Ego State Disorder, let's proceed to a description of it in action, within a setting of psychotherapy.

Chapter II
"Bob"

I'm going to try to depict what happened over several years of therapy with three men. I'll roll them into one and call the composite "Bob." First, a little history.

At the point we pick up the story, Bob had been coming for therapy for about a year. He had a number of symptoms, including headaches, food addiction, and sexual inhibition. His relationship with his parents had been rather unsatisfactory, and he had felt during childhood that an older brother was preferred over him. His parents were strict Catholics, and he had been an alter boy in the church for several years. He was a good athlete, and had won school awards in several sports. But he never seemed to have any really close friends during high school and college, including girlfriends. He had been married for about ten years to the only girl he ever dated seriously. They had no children, partly due to his queasiness about sex.

Therapy during the first year had focused mostly on his childhood, and feelings of resentment and jealousy toward the older brother, with accompanying anger toward his parents. We'll pick up on a session in which he reports a dream.

SESSION A

Bob: I had the strangest dream last night. I dreamt that I was in church, and right there, lying in a pew all by itself, was a baby in a diaper. It looked malnourished, but otherwise healthy. Now here's the crazy part: it talked to me! It was nowhere near old enough to do that, but did it anyway. I couldn't make out exactly what it was saying, but it seemed to be pleading with me to do something, like take care of it or something.

Me: How did you respond?

Bob: I felt real sorry for it, but couldn't imagine what I could do to help. So I just walked away. Made me sad.

[Bob and I had never talked about Ego States, but it seemed to me that this might be a very young Part trying to come out and make contact with him. So I told him a little about Parts, and asked if it made any sense to him.]

Bob: Well, yeah, but it also freaks me out. Are you saying I might be inhabited by more than one person?

Me: Not really. If this baby really is a Part of you, it remembers some things that were probably just too painful for you to keep in consciousness. If that's what it is, he could be extremely helpful to you, since he might know things that you need to remember. Would you like me to talk with him?

Bob: I guess so. What if he won't talk?

Me: Actually, I mostly want to talk to HIM. I doubt that he would be able to just come right out and tell us things right away. It's usually more gradual than that. I just want to ask if he IS a Part, and propose some ways that he might be able to communicate with you, to tell you what he knows, that you've repressed.

Bob: Well, okay. Give it a shot.

Me: Would you mind closing your eyes for a few minutes while I do this?

Bob: No problem.

Me: Okay, I'm now going to talk to what *might* be a Part of Bob. I'll refer to you as Little One. First of all, if you really are a Part, and have things that you want Bob to remember, would it be possible to give Bob some sign? I'll wait a few minutes to see if anything happens.

Bob: Holy cow. No need to wait. I saw him again - the same baby - and he had a big smile on his face. You realize of course that this is making me feel a little crazy.

Me: I do realize that. I'm sorry for that part of it. But I'm really glad that he's willing to communicate with us. I think you'll be amazed at how helpful he can be. What I want to suggest to him now is that we go slowly. I think he already understands that, but I want to say it out loud anyway. If he tries to push too fast he can run you right out of this office. So what I'm proposing to you, Little One, is that you show him small portions of what you need him to remember when he's dreaming. We won't have to always be limited to that, but I think for right now it will be easier for him to accept what you bring. How does that sound to you?

Bob: For chrissake, he's smiling again!

Me: How about for you - how does that sound to you?

Bob: Well, I really like the idea about going slowly. I can tell you it's going to be a little while before I can even believe that this all happened. Are you *sure* I'm not possessed?

Me: Yes, I'm sure. What you'll begin to realize as we go along is that you're not alone. Millions of people have these internal Parts, and the vast majority are just as unaware of them as you've been. If you recall, you have found other things during your therapy that you had completely repressed, and then finally remembered. I believe that this material coming from the baby is just a little more painful. Which is why it has taken longer to surface. But I think it's also vitally important to your life and your welfare. So I believe that what's happening is a good thing. You do need to be ready for some painful events to come to the surface. But you lived through them once, and you can do it again.

SESSION B

Several weeks have gone by, and Bob has had dreams about his older brother, Steve.

Bob: I had another one last night. Steve was pounding on me again, and I just took it. He was a lot bigger than me, and always able to convince Mom and Dad that I started it. This dream was different from most, though. Even though he wasn't hitting me in my back, I awoke with a terrible pain in that area. That and my shoulder were almost on fire, it hurt so bad.

Me: How would you feel about me asking to talk to the Little One again?

Bob: Why? There's no baby involved. This is just more of the same crap coming from Steve.

Me: Maybe. But the amount of pain makes me think the Little One is leading you toward some memory. Okay if I try?

Bob: Sure. Fire away. Like you said, I lived through it once........

Me: If it's okay to close your eyes, I'll address the Little One. (After a couple of minutes to let Bob relax.) Okay, Little One. I think you're trying to tell Bob something. Something involving pain in the back and shoulders. Is that right? If so, I'd like to see if you can add a little bit to help us more.

At that point Bob begins to moan, and then cry deeply.

Bob: Oh, shit. I don't know what it is, but it's going to be bad. I can tell. The baby's looking at me like he's wondering if I can handle this. He looks scared.

Me: Ask him if there is perhaps one other thing that he can add at this point. Then that should be enough for now.

Bob: I just did. He just warned me about something. I could see it in his eyes. He's really scared. (Crying). Wow, that little baby cares about me. He wants me to know what he remembers, but he doesn't want to hurt me. Jesus. This is the strangest thing I've ever heard of.

Me: Yes, I think he does care about you. I think he is a part of you, and originally came *from* you, but had to split off mostly. He is probably very happy that you'll take him seriously, and listen to what he has to say.

Bob: No problem about that. I'll have to admit though that I dread whatever is coming.

Me: I know. But I'm pretty sure he'll give you enough time to get ready.

SESSION C

Several more weeks pass, during which Bob does very little dreaming. But then one day......

Bob: It happened again. Same dream of Steve beating me up, and the same terrible pain in my back and shoulders.

Me: Sounds to me like the Little One is ready to go ahead some. Do you feel ready?

Bob: I'm not sure. Let's see. I'll close my eyes.

Me: Okay, Little One, is it time to add some more?

Several minutes pass, during which time Bob starts to twitch in his shoulders.

Bob: What in the Hell is that? Have I gone spastic?

Me: No. Just try to relax, and pay close attention to whatever is happening in your body.

Bob's face begins to distort, and the twitching increases. He is lying on his back, as usual. But suddenly his back arches in a most shocking way. The arching is so severe that it looks like his back might break!! I am quite honestly terrified. I have never seen anyone's body do such a thing. I didn't even know it *could* do such a thing! It stays in that position for close to 30 seconds, and then finally relaxes. As I finally let out a breath, the same thing happens again! Bob is moaning, a terrible guttural sound, and obviously in horrendous pain. But once again after about 30 seconds, he relaxes. I realize that I have a death grip on the arms of my chair, and try to relax as well. Bob is breathing very rapidly, but seems not to have broken his back. What a relief!

Me: Bob, are you all right?

Bob: (Barely able to speak.) Little by little. You'll never believe what just happened.

Me: Try me.

Bob: I was real little, still in the crib. Steve was about 8, and strong. He picked me up and threw me across the crib. Hard. It must have dislocated my shoulder. He did it twice. (After a long silence.) God, he wanted to kill me. All this time I was so jealous of him, it never occurred to me that he also might have been jealous of ME! I guess little babies do get a lot of attention. And it took some away from him. He couldn't stand it. (After another long silence.) Boy, this explains a few things. Why I've always been so terrified of him, even as an adult. But also why the Little One appeared to me as a baby. I WAS a baby when it happened. But you know, even after all this torture, you're right: I lived through it once, and it didn't kill me this time either.

Me: To tell you the truth, I wasn't so sure there for a while. That was some serious agony you went through.

Bob: I know. Can we stop now? Please?

Me: Sure, that's plenty for one day!

In the ensuing months, there were a number of changes in Bob's life that seemed connected with this experience. Primarily, he noticed a decline in the number of headaches that he gotten so used to. They were not altogether gone, but significantly diminished, and he was very grateful. He also said that he felt a little more confident that he was not crazy. Not that he was ever severely disturbed, but there was always a subtle sense that he didn't know who he was, or how he got to be that person.

He also felt somewhat different toward Steve. For a time he considered contacting him and telling him what he remembered, partly out of revenge. But then he realized that Steve was just 8 years old at the time. True, he did something really stupid and destructive, but he was a very young child. Bob finally felt that there was no reason to punish him further, knowing that he might feel terrible guilt over it already, if he even remembered it. At least for Bob, it was finished, and that was enough.

SESSION D

Over the next several months, Bob cancelled a number of sessions, which wasn't like him. I wondered whether perhaps the Little One (or me) had gotten too ambitious with him, and had driven him away. But then he returned with another dream.

Bob: Here's a doozy for you. I dreamed that a police officer pulled me over for speeding. As I was getting my registration out of the glove compartment, I noticed that he was unzipping his pants! That was it.

Me: So someone in a position of authority was behaving in a sexual way toward you, right?

Bob: Yeah, right. And by the way, it felt like I was getting sick just listening to you say that.

Me: Do you ever remember anything like that? An authority figure doing something sexual toward you?

Bob: Not that I can remember. But we both know that I have some sexual hangups, so there may well be something in there I don't know about.

Me: Want me to ask around?

Bob: Sure. It's what you get paid for.

Me: If you'll close your eyes, I'll ask the inside of you if there is anything they can add to the dream at this point.

Bob: (After a long pause.) Uh-oh. I just heard a voice say very loudly, "Shut up!!"

Me: I think that voice was talking to me. And I also think you're right - that this is a doozy. Sometimes when there is a really traumatic memory coming up, there will be a protective Part show up that is committed to preventing it. This Part might believe that the memory would kill you, or be terribly destructive to your life in some way. If it's okay with you, I'm going to assume that something like that is happening now, and make the protective part a proposal. To you - the Protective Part - I want to make a request. I'm pretty sure that you're dead set against this memory coming up into awareness. And I think I understand why. It must be something really awful and devastating. And I certainly commend you for wanting to protect Bob from it. But I imagine that you know who I am, and what Bob and I do together. I think you might agree that in the past when blocked memories have resurfaced that it has resulted in improvement in Bob's life. I'm fairly sure that you are convinced, however, that it is not so in this case. So my proposal is this: how about letting whoever knows about the memory have a little slack? Let him or her bring back just small segments of it at a time, so Bob has a chance to digest them. If you would be willing to try this for - say - two months, I think it would give you a chance to se if Bob could handle it or not. I trust you. If you see that it cannot work, I'll abide by your decision, and I think Bob will also. But I'll tell you something in advance: I've never had anyone quit on something like this. I doubt you'll be the first. But if you do, you have my word. We'll stop.

Bob: (Long silence.) My head feels like it's trying to shake up and down. I guess that means he'll try it.

Me: Okay. Now brace yourself. This Part knows what he's talking about, and what you're up against. It's going to be tough. Really tough.

Bob: You know what? My LIFE has been tough. And I'm real tired of it. I've seen enough benefit from what we've done so far that I'm willing to give it my best shot. I don't really have a choice anyway.

For a couple of months, Bob kept his appointments, but seemed sullen and a little depressed. He didn't seem to make much headway with anything, and considered quitting again. But then I got a call from him that he needed to come right away, even though it wasn't his usual time.

SESSION E

Me: This isn't typical for you. What's going on?

Bob: I just feel like I'm going to jump out of my skin, that's all. I've never been so agitated and nervous in my whole goddam life. You started all this, so it's up to you to get me out of it.

Me: I think my job is to help you get *through* it, not *out* of it.

Bob: I know you're right. Sorry. That's just an example of how out-of-sorts I am - you're the last person I should be jabbing at.

Me: Try to tell me about what you're feeling.

Bob: The main thing is I don't want to be in this body. It feels alien to me, like it's not really mine. I feel dirty.

Me: Does it feel like this has anything to do with that dream about the policeman - the authority figure?

Bob: For some reason, yes, it does. Just the feeling itself, not anything logical. If I visualize that guy, it gives me the willies, like I'm going to be sick.

(At this point I think I have a clear idea of where this is headed, and am biting my lip to keep from saying it out loud. I've heard this kind of sequence too many times not to have a fair idea of where it's going. But if there's one thing I've learned in 40+ years of practice, it's to keep my mouth shut at times like this, and let the patient come to the awareness in his own good time. I believe that clinicians feel this urge often, to "tell" what they see coming. It reminds me of the kid in second grade who is sure he has the right answer, and has his hand waving in the air screeching "Me, me, me!!" We want to be helpful, and we want to do things so that we can feel that we earn our money, and we also want to be right. It takes many years to realize that we're cheating the patient out of his own discovery. It delights our egos, and deprives the patient of his own insight. Not a good trade-off.) Now back to the session:

Me: How about trying to visualize the officer now. Does it feel like you can do that?

Bob. I'll try. (Silence.) Funny, he looks different now. Not all neat and prim like they usually do. He's a little messy. And - well I'll be damned - he has one of those collars that priests wear! Where did that come from? He didn't have it before.

Me: Sounds like somebody is trying to add elements of the memory. What else?

Bob: It's the collar. That's what makes me feel sick. Oboy, I want out of here really bad.

Me: Well, maybe that is enough for today. It seems to me that you're closer to what happened than when you came in here, and that's plenty good enough.

Bob: Just one other thing before I run for the door. The guy's face also changed. Started out being young, and now looks a good bit older.

Me: Probably also very important. Good for you.

SESSION F

Another extra session. He said it was urgent.

Me: Another disturbing dream?

Bob: No, this is totally different. I feel doomed. Like my whole world is going to fall apart. I don't like this at all.

Me: I've never seen you look so distraught. What's going on?

Bob: I have no idea. I hoped maybe you would know. All I know is that it feels like my life is crumbling around me. Not that anything external has changed - it's just the feeling. But the feeling is unbearable. Like it's the end of the world.

Me: Can you close your eyes? (He does) Now tell me everything you can about what you feel.

Bob: (Long silence, rapid breathing, twitching.) A couple days ago I had this image of a priest unzipping his pants. (Begins to sob uncontrollably.) No, it can't be. I'm - or *you're* - making this all up. (Deep sobbing.

Many minutes pass.) Oh my God, it WAS him. Remember my telling you how much I respected the priest at our church? It was <u>him</u>. Oh, shit.

(Many more minutes.)

Me: What was "him?"

Bob: He did it. (Softer crying, long period of silence.) He unzipped his pants....and then.......I guess you know. I can't stand it. I absolutely can't stand it. The one person in my childhood that I trusted the most!! That son of a bitch! He knew that my parents thought he hung the moon, and that they'd never believe me if I told on him. So he was safe.

Me: Did it occur more than once?

Bob: I think it happened a lot. He and I were alone a lot, and he had every opportunity. God damn him. If he were here right now I'd rip his heart out. That's what he did to me. No wonder I've had some sexual hangups!! I was always afraid that maybe I was really homosexual!

This session lasted a long time. I was glad that I had the time available.

Bob continued to work on the molestation for months after that. It really had turned his world inside-out. His family was very religious, and so was he, and this memory shook him to his very core. He was extremely angry with the priest, and with the church, for a good while. In time, he checked with some of the other alter boys to see if they had the same experience. Luckily, they had not, or did not remember if they had. So he eventually notified the local diocese, and hoped that they would do the right thing.

It's important to realize that the retrieval of this memory was not just an intellectual event - it involved intense feelings as well. That is the fundamental difference between Insight therapy and Experiential therapy. Just remembering something does very little to change anything, in my opinion. But once the feelings are connected as well, there is the opportunity for real healing and growth. Bob, today, has very few symptoms of any sort, and lives a more satisfying life.

DISCLAIMER

While all of the events reported above are true, it must be acknowledged that they are presented in a way that is a little too neat and seamless. Therapy is rarely this logical, linear, and tightly woven. For example, patients do from time to time report improvements in their lives, but those improvements are often gradual, and difficult to tie to specific therapeutic events. Also, dreams rarely follow each other in the obvious way that I depicted here, where each one seems to lead to the next in such predictable fashion. I have portrayed the work as I have in order to try to make it clear and understandable, not to make it correspond precisely to the real world. The fundamental precept - that recovery of memories and feelings from traumas that have been repressed leads to healing - is for me incontrovertible. But please understand that actual therapy is a bit more complicated than this, and quite different from one individual to another. I have, as it were, provided a skeleton of the therapy process, which looks fairly simple. In order to "flesh it out" some, I'll now try to describe some of my own therapy, and two of my own Parts.

Chapter III
My Own "Parts"

Before I discuss the therapy, I'd like to describe the role of the two primary Parts in my life, so that you can see the differences produced by each. Let's do this in reverse, starting with the "Good Mother Part."

As I'll describe below, my mother was the center of my young world. She seemed to love me unconditionally, and I felt the same toward her. As crazy as it may sound, I remember fantasizing that one day she and I would be married, and would be king and queen of the world. She complimented me constantly, and told me that friends and teachers held me in the same esteem that she did. You can imagine how eager I was to hear such glowing reports.

But there was a problem. As I heard them day after day, they formed a tape recording in my head. Any time I felt the least bit depressed, or distressed, I would simply play the tape and feel better. Whatever had made me feel depressed or distressed, however, had NOT been dealt with. I had given myself a dose of the "feel better" tapes, and ignored the problems. I was an addict. (I'm a little embarrassed to say that I still do it at times. The tapes are still there. The difference is that now I recognize what is happening, and force myself to face the real issues as soon as possible. But it is truly amazing how habit-forming something like that can be.)

So, as I'll describe below, I was a pretty happy child. I had no idea about the addiction, or what was coming. I lived oblivious in my little cocoon. What was coming was the other Part, which could be called the "Bad Mother Part."

The "Bad Mother" Part took shape during my adolescence. She had actually appeared many, many times earlier, in the form of her need for unceasing control, and making sure that I kept up a good appearance at all times, regardless of how bad I might feel. We got along very well most of the time, because I was a very compliant child. I was smart enough to see what was required, and managed to meet most of her expectations, completely unaware of what it was doing to me.

The problem we ultimately ran into was, as you might imagine, sex. I was just as delighted as any youngster to discover its wonders, and experimented with it in many ways. As she became aware of that, the axe came down. She quickly let me know that if I were going to evolve into a sexual man, she would have nothing to do with me. Somehow I had known that it would come to this. One day prior to puberty while playing the word game" Scrabble", I had been quite proud of forming the word "sexy" on a triple word space. Her look chilled me to the bone. There were other events as well that let me know that we were headed for serious trouble. I just did not know how serious it was to be.

One fatal day, she found some "men's" maga-zines that were mine. This time her look nearly killed me. Although I remember fearing that *she* might die as well. I knew without her saying a word that this was the end. I knew there was no possible way for me to grow up and be asexual, and I knew that there was no way she could ever accept it, or me. To do what she wanted, for me to be the person she demanded, I would have to surrender my soul. And no matter how much I loved her and wanted to please her, that was too much. I would not, and could not, do it.

Over the succeeding years, I tried every way I could imagine to re-connect with her, and always failed. I could remember so clearly how much I had thought that she loved me, and there was no way she would hurt me this much unless I *deserved it*. But over time, I slowly realized that I did not deserve it. Instead, there had to be something wrong with her to write me out of her life like that.

However, that realization would slip from time to time, and I would wallow for a while in the confusion of who did what to whom and why. As the torment went on, other feelings began to take shape. Each failed attempt at re-connection left a scar, and each scar resulted in more frustration, confusion, and finally, rage.

At some point I gave up. I think that was the moment of the birth of the "Bad Mother" Part. I had known about her bad aspects for a long time, but at this point there was a split: I became totally focused on them, to the near-total exclusion of any positive thoughts of feelings. After that there was no more love for her, and there were no more attempts at re-connection. Finally! The battle was over. There was instead disdain, fury, and raw hate. No more conflict, no more self-doubt or self-judging.

But the effect on my life was in many ways horri-ble. The disappointment and betrayal and rage at her bled over into my feelings toward many other peo-ple, even though I was only half aware of it. I tried my best to be "nice" and to act "normal", but slipped up often enough to make me realize that something was terribly wrong. For most of the next twenty years I was miserable. And often miserable to be around. Nobody could help me. (Although that's not 100% true. In High School I met a girl who has now been my wife for 47 years, and she, and her parents, helped me tremendously. But even their wonderful love and acceptance could not solve the core problem.) The Bad Mother Part was in control, and had become part of my bone marrow. So now we'll start with her, and how she showed up in my therapy.

THE BAD MOTHER PART:

My discovery of my own Parts proceeded in quite a different way from Bob. It began in 1965, when I first read a book called <u>The primal</u>

<u>Scream</u>, by Arthur Janov. Like many people who read it, I felt that it was about me. It described a sort of therapy in which the patient is given virtually total freedom to express whatever he or she feels. I felt that for some reason I needed that. Most of the people around me thought it was crazy, that I seemed more normal than most. I knew different, but had no idea what it was I knew. However, there was no way I could take the months off from work to pursue it, let alone afford it. So I tried to do it quickly, in a week-long session. Not at the Primal Institute in Los Angeles, but in Canada.

One part of the therapy was to get two massages. During the first one, I was lying on my back, thinking that this was sort of silly, and a waste of money. Suddenly, absolutely out of nowhere, both my arms shot straight up in the air, and stayed there. At the same time, I began crying like a baby. For no reason. Nothing the masseuse had done had anything to do with it. But there I was, sobbing, holding my arms in the air. But I wasn't "holding" them there - they were there totally on their own. I didn't <u>want</u> them to be there, but I couldn't put them down. The poor masseuse left the room, totally bewildered I think, and came back about ten minutes later, when I had finally stopped crying. Neither of us had any idea about what was happening, but we both sensed that it meant something.

I had another massage the next day, and the exact same thing happened. *Exactly*. No memories, no insight, nothing at all except feeling out of sorts and more than a little crazy. Oddly, I don't remember thinking very much about it afterward. I completed the week of therapy, and went back home. Nothing was much different.

Several years later, I met a woman who had been a patient at the Primal Institute, and hearing about her experience made me want to go all over again. I did. It was a very painful time for me and my family. It meant months away from them, and paying out money we could ill afford. I felt horribly selfish about it, but was utterly compelled to go.

[The Institute has gotten a lot of bad press, but I know that there are many good therapists there. I'm sorry that Janov has made some of the claims that he has, because I think they are exaggerated. That's too bad, because the basic idea is sound enough that it shouldn't have to be exaggerated.]

At any rate, after a few months there, I was lying quietly on my back in one of the darkened rooms, along with about a dozen other people. *It happened again.* Up went the arms, frozen in position, accompanied by gut-wrenching crying. Except this time it was different. I was not at the Institute. I was lying in a crib, with my arms upward, crying for my mother to pick me up. I was crying partly because I was extremely hungry, and partly because she was doing nothing to help me. She was standing over me, looking downward, expressionless. She was refusing to pick me up, despite the desperation she saw in me. All of a sudden I realized: she was teaching me a lesson. "Don't cry like that. Settle down. Don't be so upset. I'll pick you up when you stop crying and not before." The lesson would last most of my life. She taught me that emotional expression was only acceptable within definite limits. Crying uncontrollably was surely beyond those limits. Even for a baby who was crying because his stomach was burning with hunger, which mine was. It didn't matter. Nothing did. Control was what mattered.

She was German. In the early 20ᵗʰ century, it was stated plainly in the standard German child-rearing texts that children are instinctually wild animals. Without severe discipline, they will grow up to be monsters. What is required is daily beating, to teach them civility. Her real reasons for what she did went well beyond these texts, but she adhered to them in principle. It's not that I believe that children do not require discipline, but hers was way too severe for my well-being.

The immediate effect of regaining this memory was mostly unsettling to me. I had actively hated her for many years, always feeling guilty about it, believing that she couldn't possibly be that bad, and that I was just self-indulgent. But I hated her nonetheless. I could deny it for a time, but it always came back. It was the truth. Now I felt that I understood why. She had been a very stern influence in my life since I was a baby, even mildly sadistic at times. (This, along with being very seductive, makes for a wicked combination.) The fact of finally understanding where so many of the feelings came from gave me some relief. But it also made me realize that I was not making up the feelings out of thin air, but that they were there for good reason.

It was much later that I realized that the hatred of her had resulted in the formation of a Part within me. It knew perfectly well where the hatred came from, and was not about to give up on what it knew to be true. That Part was basically in charge of my life from about age 10 to age 30. During that time I was depressed, occasionally suicidal, and full of rage that I couldn't express or understand.

That's bad enough. But on top of it was the feeling that I couldn't possibly have a right to such feelings, because my mother loved me so very much. Because in many ways she <u>did</u>. And I knew it. Which leads us to........

THE GOOD MOTHER PART:

As I said above, my mother was the center of my world when I was small. She complimented me and doted on me. But most important was the way she looked at me. The only way I could ever describe it to myself or anyone else was that I felt I could see God in her eyes. It felt like total warmth, acceptance, and love. True, there had to be some inkling in there somewhere that the crib experience was real, and that the severe discipline was real. But the love was so overwhelming that I managed to almost forget about it totally. I was so happy most of the time that I can remember looking at other children and positively wishing for them that they could feel the way I did. It wasn't something I needed to guard jealously - there was plenty to go around for everyone. Or so I thought.

As I said above, it was during adolescence, and particularly puberty, that we parted. Once it became obvious that I could not help but grow up to be a man, she left me. It nearly killed me at the time, and was the beginning of twenty years of depression and misery. (I and my siblings are quite certain that she was molested, and had a host of sexual hang-ups because of it. But that was no help at the time. By the way, she and my father have both been dead for years, and I hope and assume that these revelations are not bothersome to them.)

About ten years after the event at the Institute, I was back in a sort of therapy. I had a number of patients who seemed to be experiencing things from past lives. They were so convincing that I decided to look into it myself. After a couple of dozen sessions, I can't say that I learned anything at all about my past lives, but I learned something about my present life that was totally unexpected.

Ever since I could remember, I had a painful tension in my groin area. It was so strong that I always assumed that one day it would kill me. Of course I learned to live with it. And by concentrating on it, I could gain some degree of relaxation. But as soon as I stopped, it was right back again. I supposed that there was muscular constriction in there that was so powerful that it was cutting off blood supply to portions of my body. And that couldn't be good. I never told a doctor about it, and never felt that there was any possible way to cure it.

One day while in one of these "past life" sessions, I was struck by a vivid image: it was my mother smiling at me. The same smile from childhood. The same warmth and acceptance and love. I was totally overwhelmed. I cried and cried and cried. Something in me loosened, and I cried some more. Although I didn't realize it at the time, I was allowing the Good Mother back into my life. In the years since the event at the Institute, I must have been unconsciously working to resolve my conflicted feelings toward her without being aware of it. Overall, I was feeling better, and the circumstances of my life had stabilized. I was ready to re-connect with her. Finally.

On the drive home, I was startled to realize that the groin tension was not there! I didn't think a great deal about it. I assumed that it would return, just as it always had, either that day or the next. It never did. There are, today, rare occasions when it rears its head. But it is always in the form of a warning - that I am making a mistake of some sort and need to get it straight. Once I attend to the problem, it disappears again. Completely. There is no way to explain how grateful I am for this change. I never thought it could happen - ever. I never thought anything *like that* could ever happen. Maybe in a religious conversion experience, but we've all seen how those usually turn out. To this day, I am deeply grateful. For all the help I've had, and especially to my family, for sticking with me.

Being a therapist has always seemed like the most natural thing in the world to me. Having had these kinds of experiences, how could I not want them for others? At odd moments during the day, I look upward and say "Thank you." I'm not sure exactly who I'm thanking up there, but it seems to be a part of the whole thing. I <u>am</u> grateful.

I hope that now you can see that there is more than one way to learn about, and deal with, Parts. My two Parts were formed in the same way as most of my patients - because of intense inner conflict. I could not love and hate my mother at the same moment. Both sets of feelings were terribly real, but could not stand each other. They each had to deny the existence or the reality of the other, and the feelings that went with them. Had each of them not been so extremely intense, I could have felt both of them during the same day, or perhaps an hour apart. But their power prevented that from happening. When one was present, the other had to be gone.

Like my patients, I had to split. I still recall a dream that I had during adulthood, while all this was going on. I dreamed that I, and a dozen or so classmates, were in a room that had lots of filing cabinets in it. We were supposed to try to find something, although it was not specified what it was. Wandering around looking on top of the cabinets, I found what I thought it was: a small dish of milk with a stainless steel cylinder standing in it. But what amazed me was that I was able to make the cylinder rise and fall by *thinking* about it, or wishing it to happen. I could make it levitate! I was so excited! I called to my classmates, and showed them how it worked. I remember that I was not "proud" of finding it - I was just happy that we all could do this magic thing now.

Then, without warning, the teacher approached. It cast a terrible pall over the room. I never saw her in the dream, but knew she was there, and her very presence ruined everything.

In the very next scene, seemingly totally disconnected, I was standing outside in the quad at Ohio State University. As I watched, I split into two parts. One part walked up toward the university library, dutifully and without emotion, like a robot. The other part disappeared off to the right. I knew that this part was the real me, the part of me I loved, and that I would never see it again. It was the saddest moment of my life. It's a dream I will never forget.

I think that for most, if not all, people who split into Parts, there is a moment in time like this. A single instant when the split occurs. Kind of like the Big Bang. Originally, there was one person, and then in a moment there is no more oneness. There are instead these separate Parts who hate one another, and fear that they will never be rejoined. It is a sickening feeling.

SUMMARY:

So after all this therapy, and these experiences, where does it leave me? What about my Parts now?

I think the main things is that they no longer hate or distrust each other, and do not engage in open conflict. Things inside are a lot quieter. Nor are they completely integrated. I'm not sure that is important or necessary. For me or anyone else.

During the time when they were widely separated, each had no access to the memories of the other, and therefore no way to understand or be sympathetic about what had happened to the other. But now, each has witnessed the other one going through what it did in childhood, and can understand much better why it would feel the way it does. That understanding is mutual, as is the acceptance. I think that one of the results of all that is my having more energy in my life. Previously, I had to spend a great deal of it mediating a sort of civil war between the two of them. Like I said, things are quieter now.

I still believe that those who have ESD Parts are in some ways lucky. Not at all because of the traumas that caused them, but because the Parts can be so instrumental in helping them to a better life. The split does not have to be permanent.

Whoever I'm talking to up there, thank you.

Chapter IV
Hypnotic Trance and
Altered States of Mind

Discussing hypnosis is made much more difficult because so many false claims have been made about it. It has been said to be the miracle cure for everything from addiction to weight loss to wart elimination. I may be prejudiced, but I don't believe it. No doubt there are people who are *ready* to stop smoking or eat less who are touted as success cases. But the actual role of hypnosis in the treatment is highly suspect. Of course, for the failures there is always the retort that they didn't continue treatment long enough, or do it right, or some such. I'm sure there are charlatans in every profession, and am afraid that psychology is no exception.

This is not to say that hypnosis is quackery. Far from it. In the hands of a conscientious professional, it can be a very effective form of treatment. But it is NOT usually quick, and probably never really easy. If it were, there would be no obese or addicted people anywhere.

One of the commonest questions about it is "Who is hypnotizable and who is not?" To start with, it must be recognized that hypnosis is a matter of degree. Some people can go easily into a deep trance and recall incidents from early childhood that are quite alarming. Others can use it to achieve a state of deep relaxation, and little more. What is the difference?

I believe it depends on the person's childhood experience, and the extent to which they have employed dissociation as a defense mechanism. If they had lots of early trauma (or even in adulthood in some cases), they became habituated to retreating into a fantasy world when things got too bad in this world. These people can be hypnotized readily, with or without our help. But for ordinary people who have had only the occasional bad experience, trance will be much more superficial, and may not seem like an altered state to them at all.

I hope it is clear that this is my own opinion, and not necessarily universally accepted. But it is very straightforward, and easily testable. I think it would make for an excellent Ph.D. thesis, and I hope some one will pursue it.

One of the other questions frequently asked about hypnosis is "Do they have to use that pendulum to get you started?" The answer is no. The fact remains the same, that some people are much more able to be hypnotized easily than others, and those people do not require any "gimmicks" at all. If you recall, in Bob's therapy, all I did was suggest that he close his eyes and relax. He did the rest. He had been dissociating most of his life, and all I had to do was give him the time and the permission to do it again.

One of the most fascinating aspects of hypnosis has to do with what Ernest Hilgard called the Hidden Observer.

THE HIDDEN OBSERVER

Hilgard (1986) has been studying hypnotic phenomena in the laboratory for over half a century. But it was a student of his who made one of the most important discoveries, dubbed "the Hidden Observer." In a classroom demonstration, Hilgard had induced hypnotic deafness in a subject. He was told that at the count of three he would become completely deaf to all sounds, and that his hearing would be restored when the instructor's hand was placed on his right shoulder. Hilgard counted to three. Loud sounds were then made close to the subject's head by banging wooden blocks together, and there was no sign of reaction. He also showed no response to the crack of a starter's pistol! Nor did he respond to students' questions.

Although there was no doubt about the temporary state of deafness, an inquisitive student asked if perhaps "some part" of the subject might be aware of what was going on. Hilgard agreed to pursue the possibility and said to the subject:

"As you know, there are parts of our nervous system that carry on activities that occur out of awareness, of which control of the circulation of blood, or the digestive process, are most familiar. However, there may be intellectual processes also of which we are unaware, such as those that find expression in night dreams. Although you are hypnotically deaf, perhaps there is some part of you that is hearing my voice and processing the information. If there is, I should like the index finger of your right hand to rise as a sign that this is the case."

To the surprise of the instructor, as well as the class, the finger rose! The subject immediately said:

"Please restore my hearing so you can tell me what you did. I felt my finger rise in a way that was not a spontaneous twitch, so you must have done something to make it rise, and I want to know what you did."

Hilgard assured him that he would do so, but that first he wanted to ask another question.

"Does the part to whom I am now talking know more about what went on?"

"Yes."

"Tell me what went on."

"After you counted to make me deaf, you made noises with some blocks behind my head. Members of the class asked me questions to which I did not respond. Then one of them asked if I might not really be hearing, and you told me to raise my finger if I did. This part of me responded by raising my finger, so it's all clear now." (Hilgard, pp. 186–187).

This part of the subject which retained its auditory acuity was labeled a "Hidden Observer." This same phenomenon has been demonstrated repeatedly under the most rigorous experimental controls. One of the most common techniques involves "hypnotic anaesthesia." The hypnotized subject places one arm in a bucket of ice water. The water is cold enough so that the ordinary person could not stand it for more than a few seconds.

In trance, however, the person seems content to leave it there for many minutes with no sign of discomfort. Once one hand is placed in the ice water, a pencil is placed in the person's other hand, and he is asked to indicate the degree of discomfort on a scale from one to ten. The numbers depict exactly what would be normally expected: at first the pain is minimal, but quickly becomes extreme. If this other part of the person is accessed verbally, it will angrily demand that the person be allowed to remove the arm from the bucket because it is damned painful!

Hilgard adds a most interesting postscript to his account of the original discovery:

"It should be noted that the Hidden Observer is a metaphor for something occurring at an intellectual level but not available to the consciousness of the hypnotized person. It does not mean that there is a secondary personality with a life of its own - a kind of homunculus lurking in the shadows of the conscious person. [It] is merely a convenient label for the information source tapped through experiments with automatic writing and automatic talking." (Hilgard, p. 188)

He may be right. There may well be cases where there is a secondary level of awareness that does not qualify as a full-blown secondary personality. But for him to imply that this is always the case seems heavy-handed to me. This may be yet another example of the kind of perceptual difference that derives from experimental, as opposed to clinical, background experience. Curiously enough, later in the same book he seems to relent this position somewhat. In describing the Watkins' (1979–1980) work with Ego States, he says:

"They described an ego state as an enduring fraction of the total personality, like a 'covert' or incipient multiple personality. The Watkins' methods yielded hidden observers in all of their subjects and patients... It is understandable that the patients should have assigned the hidden observer to one or more of these acknowledged states. *Perhaps less expected was that within the same person some ego states reported while other ego states denied that they had knowledge of the concealed pain* (or hearing in the study with the students). There are clearly some analogies between the hidden observer phenomenon and the ego-state interpretation, with both representing dissociations...... The interpretation of ego states as incipient multiple personalities is an intriguing possibility, suggesting that multiple personalities may be more prevalent than commonly believed (p. 300). [My italics]

His use of the word "incipient" is most interesting. It suggests that ego states are not stable entities in and of themselves, but are always evolving in the direction of becoming Alters in Multiple Personalities. But why should this be so? Why should they necessarily always deteriorate into a more severe form of dysfunction? Why can't ego states be simply ego states? I think it is important to remember that Hilgard wrote all this more than twenty years ago. Ego states were almost totally unacknowledged at that time. Helen and John Watkins were among the very first people to recognize and write about them. I still recall that when the diagnosis of Multiple Personality was discussed in my graduate classes at Vanderbilt University, it was dismissed with the observation that "Yes, it's probably real, but there are only a few such people in the world, and you'll never run into them, so don't pay it much attention." That was the accepted opinion throughout academia, not just at Vanderbilt. Now, here in Asheville, we have support groups for Multiples, the members of which number in the dozens. And yet to this day, the majority of clinicians whom I know do not believe in either Ego States or Multiple Personality. (I'll talk more about how and why this seems to be true in Chapter VII).

With our understanding of ESD and personality Parts, I think we are in a position to add some clarification to the enigma of the Hidden Observer. Two questions: does everyone have a Hidden Observer? And: can everyone be induced to stick their hand in ice water for minutes without complaining? I'm fairly sure that the answer to both is NO.

The man that Hilgard chose for the demonstration was someone whom he knew to be hypnotizable. He would have wasted the class time if the man were not. I'll go out on a limb and say that the Part of the man that was appealed to, in order to induce a state of deafness, was a very young Part. Small children will do almost anything to please adults whom they trust. I think that stage hypnotists, when they scour the audience for volunteers, must be looking for people who look child-like, or some such. I'm not really sure what they look for, but I'll bet they could tell you, if they would. I seriously doubt that they would choose a cynical-looking, sour-faced adult (who most likely would not be in the audience in the first place).

So if the cooperative Part is very young, who is the Hidden Observer? If you turn to the cover of this book, there he is: the man in military uniform. The Protector. The others, all trying to get to the surface to tell what they know, are younger. They are more naive, more trusting, than the Protector. It is as though they are saying "Let me out! I have information that the adult needs to hear! I can help him!" The Protector, who is aware of the anguish and misery that would be brought about by these revelations, is saying "Shut up and get back down there! I'm the one who knows the potential damage. It could kill him! He's still alive because of me, and I'm not going to let you ruin him!"

When Hilgard made contact with the Hidden Observer in the man, he (it?) was indeed angry about what was being done to the adult. The Protector has an unenviable job. He is seen by all of the Parts as the Bad Guy, the sergeant-at-arms. But there is an absolute necessity for him to be doing his job, and he knows it. If all the Parts were to clamor to the surface at once, the adult would become hopelessly psychotic, and he knows that also. So there is great antagonism between him and the other Parts. It takes a lot of time, and a lot of dialogue among them, to get to a place where they can compromise. It is only then that the Protector can allow each of them the opportunity to reveal small bits of information at a time, to allow for gradual healing.

POST-TRAUMATIC STRESS DISORDER

Another category of altered states is contained in a diagnosis called Post-Traumatic Stress Disorder (PTSD). This diagnosis is highly relevant to our purposes. It always involves events in a person's life which were sufficiently traumatic that he or she dissociated to a significant degree. Thus it always also involves a good many repressed memories. These could be due to war injuries, childhood sexual abuse, severe physical beatings, or any other things of that sort. This disorder is characterized by certain sorts of symptom formations. Nightmares are almost always present. There could be an infinitely diverse set of physical symptoms, such as headaches, paralysis, skin problems, and panic disorders. We might also expect things like depression, agitation, and sleep or appetite disturbance.

Hypnotherapy is considered widely to be the treatment of choice for PTSD. This is especially true if the trauma is fairly time-limited, as in cases like injuries sustained in war, or automobile accidents. The procedure is deceptively simple, although by no means painless. After induction, the person is encouraged to recall the specific events that led up to the trauma. As he does this, he will gradually begin having the same bodily and emotional reactions that he had during the event(s).

A little at a time then, he is able to bring back into consciousness portions of the experience that were repressed, until finally the entire event is experienced.

Note that I say "experienced" and not "re-experienced". There is a common misconception about therapy that asks "Why re-experience misery? It was bad enough the first time - why bring it up again." The answer is because portions of it never *were* experienced. By the body - yes, by the conscious mind - no. In treatment, they are being experienced for the first time in full awareness. Following this, we can expect various symptoms to gradually diminish and then hopefully disappear altogether.

DISSOCIATION: DEATH AND REBIRTH OF A CONCEPT.

Dissociation, like the Phoenix, is coming back to life. It flourished nearly a century ago, serving as the cornerstone of most psychological theories. Janet (1907), Prince (1906) and others felt that human behavior and thought were not determined by some single source, but rather by a wide variety of sources. Some of these were thought to be conscious while others were either co-conscious or not conscious at all. Hypnosis was popular as a psychological treatment, and it was taken for granted that many "states of mind" were possible in people.

The demise of the concept was due in the academic world to the rise of a theory called Behaviorism. Behaviorists were convinced that if something was not empirically verifiable, it was not worth paying serious attention to it. That dealt a serious blow to dissociation because at the time we did not know how to demonstrate its existence in the laboratory.

The rebirth began much sooner in the public consciousness than in professional psychology. The popularity of the books and movies Sybil and The Three Faces of Eve made it apparent that the idea of multiple layers of awareness struck a chord in the lay psyche. Once again, the first professionals to acknowledge it were hypnotherapists, probably because they witnessed the layering consistently in their work. Gradually, it has snuck back into the thinking and writing of many clinicians. As recently as 15 years ago, there were very few psychiatric hospitals or mental health organizations that had established treatment programs for dissociative disorders. Today, it is hard to find one that does *not* have such a program. There is at least one professional periodical that focuses specifically on the topic (entitled <u>Dissociation</u>) and there may well be others in the works.

Coming full circle, it has made its way into the laboratory. Psychologists have done an impressive series of studies on something they call Implicit Memory. While interpretations of the results vary, the basic idea is that we learn and retain a lot more than we are immediately aware of. Under the right circumstances, we are able to call up this information that we had no idea was in our heads. Meanwhile, neuroscientists are taking the notion of Multiple Personality seriously, and are finding that various means of tracking brain activity show dramatically different results when different Alters are present.

Chapter V
Dreams

Among the various sorts of dreams that occur, at least three are important in ESD therapy.

1. Strategy dreams. These dreams are about important events in our daily lives, such as impending exams, having surgery, deciding whether to adopt a child, etc. This is when we practice "lucid dreaming." We try out one solution or strategy, perhaps find it inadequate, and then alter it to see if the outcome is better. We can do some excellent problem solving in these dreams.

2. Repressed trauma dreams. The content is what one would expect. These usually bring up feelings associated with the early experience, and are more often referred to as nightmares.

3. Dreams about Ego States. These dreams inform us when a particular Ego State is trying to make its presence known, as well as the internal changes

and power struggles that go on in the unconscious among the States.

Let's consider some examples of each, and how they can be used in therapy. First, strategy dreams:

Paul had a dream that he had an important physics exam the next day, but overslept and as a result failed the course. One of the things we had learned about him was that he had a tendency to self-destruct and undermine himself. He was exceptionally bright and had the capacity to be a top-level student. But we knew that he also carried, from childhood, a great sense of shame and worthlessness. So he occasionally placed one foot directly in front of the other and fell flat on his face. On the ground face-down was where he felt like he really belonged.

He really was facing a physics exam the next day, so there was some urgency to the situation, and we took the dream as a warning. Once he was in a trance, I asked a Part inside to help us. I suggested that we might strike a deal. If he would help Paul on the exam tomorrow, I would promise him extra time during the next session to tell us whatever he wanted. He found this acceptable, and Paul passed the exam with good marks.

My thinking was that this exam was important for the rest of Paul's life, and that this Ego State was not mature enough to realize the consequences that would ensue if he overslept, or performed poorly. I hoped that, in time, as the sense of shame receded, all of him would be glad of this intervention. But this was fairly early in my career. It seemed to turn out well at the time, but I would handle it differently now. In general, I almost never intercede directly in people's lives. The next example tells why very clearly.

Joan was a wife, a mother of two adolescents, and a full-time nurse. She was a highly responsible person who could be relied upon by everyone she dealt with. However, she found it difficult to take care of herself or her own needs. During therapy, we accessed a Part called Joanie who was quite young and who liked more than anything to sing silly songs, just for fun.

At some point, I got the not-so-bright idea to invite Joanie to participate more in Joan's life, so as to offset the drudgery of caring for everyone but herself. What I suggested was that whenever Joanie sensed that Joan was overloaded with responsibility, she sing a silly song inside her head to remind her of what she was doing. This sounded innocent enough to me

(I was still pretty new at this.) The next day I received a phone call from Joan. She was frantic. Apparently Joanie felt that Joan was over-responsible nearly all the time, and had been singing silly songs in Joan's head the entire day! You can easily imagine how difficult it would be to be a competent nurse when you can't think straight because of some ridiculous song going on forever inside your head! I quickly begged Joanie to stop, and made the same trade-off to give her more time in session if she would do so. She did, but it certainly taught me a lesson: Don't Take Sides! The balance of power among the Parts is so complicated and constantly shifting that you have no idea what the consequences will be. A short-term gain may turn out to be a long-term debacle and can lead to a serious loss of trust.

As far as dreams dealing with repressed trauma, you can refer to the chapter on Bob to see how these work. That leaves us with dreams about Ego States:

Mary dreamed that a man, a woman, and a child were pursuing her, and that she was going to have to be violent to get rid of them. She somehow got the woman down on the floor, but the woman kept twisting her head toward Mary to make her look at her face.

The faces of all three - a family - were very ugly, with deformed features, terrible complexions, and with loose skin hanging around their faces. Otherwise, their bodies seemed normal. When she awoke, she wasn't sure whether or not she had killed the woman, but she knew that she wanted to.

Mary had come to therapy with the conviction that her early life had been fine. Her reason for coming was that she didn't seem to get along with most people very well, and she wanted to work on that. In time, she discovered that there was a connection - that her early life had something to do with her lack of friends.

This dream was the first time we were introduced to Parts representing her mother, father, and a Part of herself as a child. They were all things she had spent her life refusing to see. That is why in the dream the mother Part kept forcing Mary to look directly at her - to see the truth. She wanted to be acknowledged, to finally be recognized for who she really was and what she remembered. Mary, in turn, wanted to kill her so that she could remain oblivious to what really happened in the family.

The reason for the loose skin was that her parents were obese. Even though she never was overweight, she always felt that she should be, by kinship. In fact, she became anorexic for a time to protect against that body image. The dream message was "Here we are. It's time for you to see who we <u>really</u> are."This is one of the ways that Ego States are most often introduced. They are dreamt about as forcing their way into the person's perceptual field in some way. Usually the person responds as Mary did, by trying to kill them or at least drive them away, back into the unconscious.

Many of these dreams depict the person being assaulted or attacked by monsters or ugly creatures who turn out to represent those things the person has never been able to face. An adolescent in treatment used to dream of being chased by huge, terrible monsters through big-city streets in which there no people, and no one to help him. He would wake up in a horror, certain that they meant to kill him. But little by little, he realized that they were not trying to kill him at all, but just to force him to face things that had been previously unbearable in his life. I encouraged him, at some point when he was ready, to turn around and actually look at them, which he had never done. It was then that he began to see that the expression on their faces was not nearly as menacing as he had assumed. He had been running so hard and so fast that he had never had the opportunity to look at them at all. Gradually, as he came to grips with what they needed for him to see, the nightmares faded, and his overall level of fear diminished greatly.

ERRORS IN DREAM INTERPRETATION

One of the things that has taken me the longest to learn is to NOT try to interpret someone else's dreams. Instead, I now ask the Part that has created the dream to talk about it. Let me give an example of how this change came about.

One man dreamed of being entirely alone at the beach. There were other people there, but they stayed a great distance from him. He felt a curious longing for some specific things, but could not identify what they were. I felt sure I knew what they were. This dream was plainly about existential loneliness, with him longing for intimacy, etc., etc. Luckily, I for some reason kept my mouth shut, because it turned out I was dead wrong.

In trance, one of the Parts gave a totally different meaning, which both the man and I recognized to be true as soon as we heard it. This man had a drinking problem. While he was not a true alcoholic, he had relied on it much of his life to give him relief from his difficulties. He had recently tried for the first time to give it up completely. He had then proudly reported that he wasn't nearly so dependent on it as he had feared he might be. But the Ego State that did the talking (in his head) said that he was really tired of the drinking and all the trouble it caused him. He was in fact not finished with the drinking at all. In the dream, he sent him away to a beach where he had no drinking companions and no one to distract him from facing the truth. As soon as he heard that, he realized that he had indeed felt a craving for alcohol that he had not admitted to himself. This gave him a much clearer picture of what he was really up against, and a much greater chance for success in dealing with it.

The dream was helpful to him in facing up to his dependency. It was helpful to *me* in facing up to my arrogance. Given the amazing complexity of the mind, it embarrasses me to think that I might have ever thought I could read someone else's thoughts and feelings in their dreams. As I said earlier, one of the great advantages of having Ego States is that you can ask them directly about many things that you might otherwise find very difficult to uncover.

Chapter VI
Sexual Abuse

"If only there were evil people somewhere insidiously committing evil deeds, and it were necessary only to separate them from the rest of us and destroy them. But the line of dividing good and evil cuts through the heart of every human being. And who is willing to destroy a piece of his own heart?"

(from the Gulag Archipelago, Solzhenitsyn, 1973)

When I first became acquainted with the reality of sexual abuse more than forty years ago, I firmly believed that all perpetrators should be lined up and shot. I was seeing the life-long effects of what they had done purely for their momentary pleasure, and the unspeakable misery and suffering of their victims resulting from it. Shooting them seemed to be letting them off too easy, but was the only thing that came to mind.

However, time does change things. I now understand, along with Solzhenitsyn, that it is not that simple.

Many of the perpetrators have themselves been abused as children, and part of their "pleasure" is actually a feeling of revenge. To make matters worse, for many years it was not universally recognized that the effects would be so devastating to the children. I think many perpetrators naively assumed that there would be no serious repercussions because the child was so young, and could not possibly remember anything about it. No, I am not in any way making excuses for them. Certainly not in this day and time. Everyone knows that there are laws relating to abuse that have put thousands of adults behind bars. And when they are released, they are identified and kept track of, and societies know where they are and where they are going before they even get there.

But for so many centuries, sexual abuse of children was a secret that was not revealed in decent societies. When Freud first found it in his patients, he reported it as it was reported to him. But very soon he was silenced. Society labeled him a pervert, and shamed him for making any such outrageous claims. He was suggesting that molestation was occurring in some of the best European families! That would never do.

Finally, the pressure put on him was so severe that he reneged. He basically claimed that the reports of molestation were really fantasies in the minds of children, which were powerful enough to seem like real memories to them as adults. He may have thus done the same thing to his patients that was done when they were very young: told them they were wrong, that the fault was <u>theirs</u>, and they needed to accept and get over it.

But as Schultz (1990) observes, "it must be noted that Freud never denied that the childhood abuses his patients reported *might* have occurred. What he did deny was his earlier view that they *always* occurred." But there was also a retraction that Schultz might have missed. "Such widespread perversions against children are not very probable," Freud wrote (Freud, 1985, p. 264). Apparently, the tip of the iceberg had been sighted and then quickly discounted. It has taken more than one hundred years for us to run solidly aground on it.

For reasons that I do not fully understand, sexual abuse is a uniquely powerful kind of trauma. Even in cases where the adult has done nothing to physically hurt the child, there is nonetheless a feeling on the part of the youngster of being sorely wounded and viscerally sickened, far beyond what logic might have predicted. They usually perceive it as *themselves* having violated the very basic rules of social decency, of having committed a crime so grievous that they can never again be washed clean.

I have been surprised to see this reaction in children who are pre-verbal, prior to about 16 months of age. It makes me wonder if the response is instinctual, and has little or nothing to do with "learning" about social taboos. Somehow they have this gut reaction long before they could possibly have known about social mores in any cognitive manner.

There has been ongoing debate within the sciences for many decades about something called "genetic memory." The question is: Are we born with certain kinds of knowledge, or talents, or instincts accumulated by our ancestors? In sports, music, and many other arenas, there are children who show abilities that are amazing, completely out of the ordinary, and often their parents had been gifted in the same areas.

Also, where do phobias come from? Why are some people who have had no known contact with snakes, spiders, or whatever terrified of them? One wonders if there was a period of human history when snakes and spiders etc. were so prevalent that they posed a serious threat to human existence. Many clinicians who have dealt with sexual abuse have wondered the same thing about it. Has it caused enough misery and anguish over the course of history that it now is experienced by children as instinctually very, very bad? Is that why so many patients remember it as having had a "feeling in their bones" about how disgusting and awful it was?

HOW EASILY IT CAN OCCUR:

I offer the following example not to make parents even more paranoid about sexual abuse than they might already be, but to illustrate just how easily it can occur. I know well the power of denial, and how strongly we are inclined to assume that this sort of thing always happens to "someone else."

Helen was four when it happened. Her family was on vacation. Her mother had taken her younger sister shopping - just down the street. She and her dad were getting ready to take a nap. Prior to that, he was tickling her as he often did, on her tummy. He would pretend that his fingers were running around, and would eventually fall into a pool - her belly button. It was all totally familiar. Except this time she noticed that the tickling game seem to make his "peepee" rise upward, and she was of course curious about it. How could a little girl not be curious about something that at first just laid there, and then gradually assumed a life of its own and rose into the air? Even though he had on boxer shorts, it was clear what was happening. She didn't exactly want to look, but it was fascinating. Then he noticed where she was looking, and he did something he had never done before. He suggested that it would rise even higher if she touched it. She thought something like "Wow! How amazing that would be that just touching it would make it come to life even more. Okay, I'll try it!"

And so she touched it, and sure enough it rose higher. In trance, as an adult, she remembered everything changing after that. Several things happened. For one thing, she remembers a feeling in her private parts that was very good, and yet frightening at the same time. But more importantly, she noticed a change in her daddy. His breathing became faster, and he had the strangest look on his face. But what she sensed mostly was that the tickling was no longer fun at all, but made her feel like throwing up. She wanted to stop. But he was enjoying himself a lot, and she felt bad about making him quit. He suggested that she take off her swimsuit so he could see *her* peepee. She did so very reluctantly. He should have sensed at that point that something was wrong, and that what he was doing was wrong. But he was aroused, and men think only poorly, and almost exclusively of themselves, at those times.

Luckily, it was at that moment that her mother and sister returned from shopping. What a relief! Unfortunately, however, it did not end there. Helen lived the next eight or nine years feeling that she was constantly being hunted down by him. He allowed her no privacy at all, and the abuse got much worse. If he were anywhere around, she stayed tied up in knots of tension. He of course knew exactly how to ensure that she never told anyone. Until almost thirty years later. A long time to keep a secret. His death eventually made the telling a little easier.

What is so striking to me about this story, and that of many other persons, is how "innocently" it begins. It is a hot summer day, and a grown man is left alone with a sweet young girl. She does what any young girl would do. It is fun, and seems totally natural. But it soon leads to this terrible conclusion. I sometimes wonder - did he even mean for it to happen? He didn't seem to have done anything similar to her older sister. Why Helen? Did he feel closer to her? Did he honestly think she would not be damaged by what he did? I believe that some abusers are probably later shocked and ashamed of what they do. For some of them, it is a one-time event, and they never do it again. They too sense that "something is wrong", and are able to stop themselves from repeating it.

SYMPTOMS OF SEXUAL ABUSE

However innocently it might begin, sexual abuse is usually so traumatic that it leads to the formation of many symptoms. The first is often a far-away look in the child's eyes. She may seem dazed, inattentive, and lethargic. Unfortunately, she may look almost exactly like this when she is getting a cold or the flu, and we are much more likely to think of those things than of abuse. However, if she has been abused, the symptoms will probably not go away completely, and will recur even after some time when they have temporarily disappeared.

The child will almost always try hard to stay away from the abuser. Of course this behavior can also seem normal enough. There can be a hundred reasons why a child would want to avoid certain people. But this is a time to ask questions: Why? Did something happen? Is there something you're afraid to tell me?

Children who have been abused almost always change in noticeable ways. Granted, they will gripe and complain about being questioned frequently, and clearly do not want to talk about abuse at all. But I think that educating them about it in a way that is consistent with their age and ability to understand is the best form of prevention. And being occasionally questioned about unusual behavior on their part is just something they have to live with.

I have been struck with the ingenuity that children show in their dissociative responses to abuse. One woman learned to focus so hard on the sounds within her ears that she could actually hear the blood flowing around in there. She had no idea that there was anything abnormal about this until one session when bad memories were flooding back in. Suddenly there it was, the focus on her inner ears, and the relief that was associated with it.

Some children learn to distort the shape of their eyeballs in order to not see what they are witnessing. They often report becoming intrigued by all the shapes and colors that result when you tighten your eyes and hold them that way for a long time. Once again, the intrigue carries them away from the pain. Unfortunately, many of these people seem to damage their eyes in the process, and have to wear corrective lenses in later life. They also tend to have chronic pain in the area of their eyes that is unaccountable for in any purely physical way.

In the course of treatment, people often discover things about their sexual tastes and habits that derive from the abuse. Sadism and masochism are good examples, as is exhibitionism.

There is another symptom of sexual abuse that is much more prevalent for girls than for boys, and that is promiscuity. Girls who have been molested, despite all the pain, become well aware that they are sexually desirable. Many of them come to feel that is their only asset. They are otherwise worthless. So why not use sex as a way to be liked? Their innocence is long gone anyway, so why not take the easy road to popularity? Young (as well as much older) boys find them very attractive, and fall all over themselves vying for their attention and sexual favors. This fact is not lost on the girls. They come to enjoy being able to maneuver the boys like so many puppets. The boys are convinced that it is sex the girls are after. Hardly. The sex itself is an afterthought, and usually something that is enjoyed little or not at all. They like being liked, and the resulting attention. For many, it is the sense of power that drives them, and the sweet taste of revenge. They get to control and make fools out of the gender that did it to them.

I do not mean to portray these girls as sexual power-mongers. It is not as though they adopted this position willfully. It is something that was forced on them, and a behavior that they carry out robot-like. There is very little real power in it, and very little real satisfaction. But some is better than none.

Some men also become promiscuous as a result of abuse. But so what if a young boy lets it be known that he is sexually available? Who cares? What young boy isn't? However, for the ones who are abused, it's different. They often become utterly preoccupied with sex, to the detriment of the rest of their lives. Love comes to equal sex. But if that is all it equals, imagine what they are missing. They usually become sexual addicts, and their lives are entirely dominated by it. They can become male prostitutes, and confined to the misery of that world. Sex is not a pleasure, but something they MUST have in order to stave off terrible feelings and memories. It's not optional, or occasional. Otherwise the pain would quickly become unbearable.

TRIGGERS:

One of the things that happens to people who are abused, or traumatized in any severe way, is that they develop "triggers." These are things that are connected with the original abuse, and threaten to bring it up into consciousness. They can be anything. Smells, colors, sounds, a look in someone's eyes, and many more things can be triggers. These people always learn to recognize them, and go to great lengths to stay as far away from them as possible. As we have seen, though, if there are the expected personality Parts associated with them, the Parts will be wanting the person to confront them. So once again there is the ambivalence - the Part pushing for awareness and the Protector insisting on safety and calm.

I cannot help but think that the current media exposure of sexual abuse might have some enduring value. When I see the way it destroys people's lives, and the way it has continued for so many years, I wonder if it is not one of the greatest dangers we face.

My worst fear is that it might somehow go undergound again. I know that seems impossible. But when I witness the incredible power of denial in people, I am not so sure. There are so many forces in our society and in ourselves that make us want to close our eyes and ears to it. It is so ugly, and so sickening, that it is natural for us to want to dissociate from our awareness of it. I hope we have the strength no to.

I also believe that our awareness of it can be very helpful in doing psychotherapy. I know that when I first started, it was never mentioned, except as being a "quirk of those remote Appalachian people." It was laughed about, and treated lightly. It was not until I treated my first case of it that I learned there was nothing funny about it, and that it was most certainly not limited to remote Appalachia. In my work previous to that, there often seemed to be "holes" - things that did not add up, pieces that did not fit, regardless of the time and effort put into the work. So when it finally came to the light of day, it was actually a relief, and seemed to offer great promise for the future.

Needless to say, attention to it also went somewhat overboard. One of the first questions asked by therapists was "Were you molested?" It quickly became seen as the #1 issue in therapy, and one that demanded immediate attention. Dozens of different types of therapy have developed with abuse as the central focus. There are treatment centers all over the country for it. For a while, adults who were accused of it, even decades later, were automatically considered to be guilty.

That then gave rise to the reaction of "False Memory Syndrome", which rightfully asserts that not all memories are truthful or accurate. So we now are struggling with all this, trying to separate truth from fantasy. It could hardly be more important that we do so. People's lives are at stake, from both points of view.

But at least the issue is up on the table, as opposed to under the rug.

In closing this chapter, I want to share a poem written by a patient, which sums it up beautifully:

I'll sue you in a court of law.
I'll tell them what you did.
How you touched and fondled me
When I was just a kid.

I'll raise my hand and take the oath
And swear that I won't lie.
Then I'll take the witness stand
And start to testify.

I'll tell them first about your games -
How you made your penis wiggle,
And how to buy a little time
I'd stare at it and giggle.

I'll tell them how your eyes were glazed,
How you'd lick your lips and smile.
I'll duplicate the way it looks
To molest a little child.

Then I'll tell them how it felt
When suddenly I knew
That you were doing something
That a decent dad wouldn't do.

I'll show them how I closed my eyes
And hung my head in shame,
And how, because it felt good,
I took on all the blame.

Then I'll repeat the scary threats -
You told me I was bad.
You told me I would go to jail
For what I did to dad.

I'll tell them how I cried at night,
Of how my heart was broken,
I'll pour out all the secrets
That I've never ever spoken.

I'll tell them how you could have been
The best dad in the world

If only you'd treated me
Like a precious little girl.

When I have told them everything
I'll simply rest my case.
I'll leave you stripped before them
With guilt upon your face.

I'll smile as you sit - beaten -
Before the angry crowd.
And when the judge says guilty,
You'll hear me laugh out loud.

I'll dance as they haul you away
To lock you in that cell,
And know when next you leave it -
You'll find yourself in Hell.

Chapter VII:
Ego States in Literature

Once I finally became convinced of the reality of Ego States (which took quite a while), I became curious about whether they had been described in literature. I soon found that they were nearly everywhere.

In a book called <u>The Split Self from Goethe to Broch,</u> Peter Waldeck (1979) lists half a dozen authors and poets from Germany alone who have written about it. He finds a consistent theme:

"The present split self is quite specific in its definition. The basic pattern remains close to the following: A childhood self....possesses the ability to love, but is oppressed by paternal influence and is juxtaposed to an adult self who possesses full emancipation from the father but lacks the ability to love. Each self thus possesses what the other needs and lacks what the other has. Both selves strive ambivalently - and only on an underlying level, not in explicit, conscious terms - for unity." (Pp. 18–19)

At first glance, this sounds rather unlike what I have described, for two reasons. First, there is special emphasis on the role of the father, whereas I maintain that both parents are equally important. All these authors lived in nineteenth-century Germany, where fathers ruled the roost and severe physical discipline was the norm. Thus when it came to squelching some facet of childhood personality, it was usually the father who was the villain.

Second, Waldeck seems to imply a split into only two parts, whereas I have often seen more than that. But it turns out that some of the authors actually described three, four, and even five parts. So this difference is not crucial. One other minor difference is that most of the fictional characters were male. All of the authors felt that their writing was inevitably autobiographical, and all happened to be male.

What is much more striking, however, is the amount of similarity. For all the authors, the essential splitting process occurs during childhood and is always a reaction to trauma. The most common trauma has to do with the father strongly condemning some aspect of the child's emotional life. Sometimes this has to do with a budding assertiveness, sometimes with a strong affection for the mother, and sometimes a visible "weakness" and "unmanliness" on the part of the child. In each case, the child must force himself to cease and desist in any display of those characteristics. Eventually, he must make himself "forget" that he ever had any such feelings or inclinations.

It is at this point that the actual split takes place. But as Carl Jung notes:

"It is a basic psychological principle that a part of the psyche split off from consciousness only *appears* to be inactivated, but in reality leads to an *obsession* of the personality, whereby the latter's goal-setting behavior is falsified in the sense of the split-off part. Thus when the childlike condition of the collective soul is repressed to the point of total exclusion, the unconscious content assumes control over the conscious goal-setting, whereby the realization of the latter is inhibited, falsified, or even destroyed. Healthy progress only comes into being through the cooperation of both." (My italics)

This rather difficult passage conveys a critical point: Not only does the repressed feeling or behavior not cease to exist, but actually now exerts a powerful influence over thought and action via *unconscious* means. We then find ourselves doing and saying and feeling things that make no sense - things that even seem contradictory to what we ordinarily think of as our true intentions. In some sense, it is this final sense of confusion, of contradictory purposes, that lies at the heart of all neurosis. It is often how we first become aware that something is wrong with us.

Another similarity between the authors' and my accounts has to do with the loss of ability to love. In every novel surveyed, the adult becomes unable to love or be loved. Somehow, when portions of the child personality are banished, they take with them into exile their loving capacities. Even though the adult body continues to live, and possibly even to thrive physically, there is always a certain numbness, and a lack of *joie de vivre*. It seems that life can only be fully experienced when the personality Parts are all present, and acting in cooperation with each other.

One of Schiller's (1953) split characters, Karl,

"...is torn between the desire to regain love (and, more broadly speaking, a divine gift of life itself) and the compulsion to dissociate himself from Franz (the adult part). ....Amalia (his mother) has given Karl the chance to return to her as the whole son, including the Franz personality. But to accept Amalia's love now would be to reintegrate the self and to take responsibility for all of Franz's monstrousness. Karl must choose between a larger (if extreme) compass of human qualities and his moral integrity."

Once again, there is the fundamental struggle to own all of ourselves - even those parts which have been branded socially undesirable or repugnant. This does NOT mean that we should act on every jealous, hateful, or murderous feeling that comes into our awareness, but only that we should acknowledge the feeling in our consciousness. The more we are split, and the less we are aware of all aspects of ourselves, the more likely we are to behave poorly, and to come across as phony when we try to act simply according to social convention.

Chapter VIII
A journey of discovery:

In order to follow this account, you will need to travel back in time with me about twenty-five years. And you have to pretend that you know nothing about Ego States. Because I didn't either. Before the journey......

Around 1985, I met a man who knew a good deal about hypnosis - something that had always intrigued me, but which I had never pursued. He told me about one woman who had been referred to him because of paralysis in both arms. Numerous physical exams had revealed nothing helpful, and she had not benefitted from physical therapy. Someone suggested that she see him for hypnosis.

Trance was easily induced , and the woman worked her way back to a recent tragedy - seeing her only son killed in a car accident. Even though it was clear to her that he was dead, she had wanted to hold him in her arms one more time before he was taken away. Because of the gruesome shape he was in, the paramedics did not allow it, and had restrained her from doing it. But in trance, the therapist suggested that she could do it now. She could imagine holding him in her arms for as long as she wanted. Her grief poured out, and she cried until she could not cry any more. When she "awoke", she was astonished to find that she had regained the use of both of her arms.

I did not doubt the veracity of his account, partly because I knew him to be impeccably honest, and also because I had heard of and seen other similar incidents. Granted, this was a fairly simple case: the trauma took place in adulthood, and was relatively easily resolved. It stood to reason that hypnosis could be an excellent tool in such a case. I considered it a good lesson, and then it all passed from my mind. Imagine my surprise, then, when a few weeks later I heard myself say to a patient "What do you think about trying a little hypnosis?"

I no more than got the words out of my mouth than a voice inside my head said "Do WHAT?!! You don't know the first thing about how to go about it!"

As luck would have it, the patient (having apparently not heard the internal clamor) said "Sure. Why not?"

Actually, I did know a little bit about it, although I had never tried it. I knew that it had to do with getting relaxed and somehow accessing lower levels of consciousness. So I figured maybe I could wing it. Besides, after so many years of clinical work, I felt that I knew a good deal about the workings of the unconscious, and that was after all what we were supposed to be dealing with. But one of the glaring things I did NOT know was what to say, how to start - those magical incantations that you are supposed to use to get things rolling.

Before the next session with the person, I visited the local library and learned a little more about it. So that when he arrived, I had a bit of mumbo-jumbo available to get it going. "Close your eyes. Now imagine you're going down some steps....deeper..deeper."

I droned on for a few minutes, feeling like a fake the whole time, hoping he wouldn't notice. However, it finally dawned on me at some point that something was happening to him. He was quite still, and his breathing had slowed considerably. I sensed that we had gotten over the first hurdle. But what now? I had never thought that I could really hypnotize anyone, and never considered what to do next. However, he seemed quite content to just lie there, and it gave me time to come up with something. So I suggested that he look for some image that would tell us about his current life - something about what he was feeling that we might not be exactly aware of. To my surprise, he did it quite easily. We pursued the image for about 15 minutes, and it seemed worthwhile.

But something much more intriguing was happening simultaneously with this. As he was talking, his right index finger was twitching, only at certain times. I had worked with this man for a good while, and had never seen his fingers twitch. It seemed to occur in response to some of my questions.

By this time, I was probably caught up in the mystique of actually having hypnotized someone and allowed my thoughts to travel a new course. I asked if he was aware of the twitching and he said no. I then asked if he would mind my trying something. He shuddered slightly and again said no. I then spoke directly to the finger that was doing the twitching, and asked if it wanted to respond to the questions. It twitched!

By now I was nearly in a trance myself. This was totally unfamiliar ground for me, and I was a little fearful. Nonetheless, I suggested a code: the finger would twitch only if the answer to the question were yes. Otherwise, it would remain still. I asked it that sounded all right, and it twitched.

We then went back over many of the same questions that I had been asking about his life, his marriage, and his children. This time the answers were different. They were less positive, but seemed more believable. In general, the responses indicated more depression and distress than he had previously owned up to.

By this time, besides being excited, I was confused. Exactly who was this that was doing the twitching? And why would it possibly be more honest than the man himself?

Being afraid to push any farther, I counted upward from ten to one, and soon he was fully conscious. I immediately asked if he was aware of what was happening. He said yes, and did not seem nearly as disturbed about it as I was. I then asked if he was controlling the finger, and he said no. That was NOT what I was hoping to hear.

He did acknowledge that the responses to my questions were probably a bit more honest than he had been able to be. But he did not like the fact that the finger seemed to have a mind of its own. It made him feel that he was not in control of himself, and that was not good. What surprised me the most was that he asked to do hypnosis again at some later date. Despite the uneasiness, he sensed that there might be some value in it.

We did it many more times, and I also began doing it with other patients. There almost always seemed to be some good come of it. So it would be only natural that I would get more training in it, and begin to use it regularly, right?

Wrong. Apparently it scared me much more than I realized. I had all sorts of rationalizations for why I stopped, and my patients mostly accepted them. But the truth is I was scared. I just didn't know it.

Then about a year later, I again heard myself say to a patient "Want to try a little hypnosis?" Once again it was too late - the words were out. And of course, yes, they were willing to try it.

This time I found myself beginning differently. Instead of trying to "induce" a trance, I just suggested that they close their eyes and pay attention to their breathing. I was then quiet until they chose to speak, and it worked fine.

(If you close you eyes in a relaxed setting and concentrate your attention on your breathing, it brings into sharper focus everything that is going on inside your body. It's a lot like focusing a microscope: you begin to see things you did not see before, with greater clarity. You may well become aware of the beat of your heart. Little by little, you can feel every beat in your fingertips and temples. For some reason, becoming focused in this way tends to lead directly to a better focus on emotions.)

Once again, the results were promising. I became so convinced of its value that I encouraged almost all my patients to try it, and most of them used it for part or all of their sessions.

Soon, however, another disturbing event occurred. Just as I had "found myself" talking to the man's finger when it twitched, now I sometimes "found myself" talking to different characters in patients' dreams. And if that weren't strange enough, they started talking back to me!

On most occasions, the voice talking to me sounded exactly like the patient's. But on other occasions it did not. It was discernibly different. Fortunately, I had in the meantime worked some with Multiple Personalities, and was partially prepared for this. But I could tell that these voices were not sufficiently alienated from the adult patients to be Alters. So I just referred to them as Parts.

Meantime, I was getting very nervous. Again. None of the psychologists I knew and talked with had any experience with Parts in these ways. They were nowhere to be found in any of the textbooks I had studied in graduate school, and I could find nothing similar in the scientific literature, despite exhaustive searching. Now, if the sky looks clear to you and twenty other people tell you it's cloudy, what are you to think? How could you alone believe that you are seeing something that dozens of other competent professionals are missing? I felt very isolated and more than a little bit foolish. I'm sure I would have abandoned the notion if it had not been for encouragement from my patients. They were convinced it was real.

Still, this subject matter was so slippery and so difficult to describe or explain that I often lost confidence in it altogether. I went through many months being quite sure that I was wrong and feeling that I should stop forcing the viewpoint on unsuspecting patients. I wrote hundreds of pages of notes, not with any intention of writing a book, but just to help me grasp this puzzling phenomenon that would not leave me alone. I was confused, frustrated, and sometimes even angry about it. Angry at the world for giving me no affirmation. But mostly angry at myself for being unwilling to abandon it.

Then one day an acquaintance loaned me a tape on hypnosis. The title said something about "Ego States", which I had never heard of. I played it none-theless. As I listened to a man named Dr. Watkins describe the theory behind it, my heart started rac-ing. It sounded somewhat like what I had been see-ing! In it, he hypnotized a college student. Presently, a Part of the student introduced itself in a slightly dif-ferent voice as "The Old One," saying that it provided a stabilizing force in his life. I squealed! I ran into the house shouting to my wife that perhaps I wasn't crazy after all - that someone else had seen the same thing!!

I couldn't rest until I had the phone numbers of these people - John and Helen Watkins - a married couple.

I talked with both of them the same day, and cannot begin to describe the relief I felt. It turned out that they were doing a workshop in Nashville a few weeks later. I attended, and served as a volunteer subject in a demonstration by Helen. Everything they said paralleled my experience almost exactly. And it turned out they had been at it for almost fifteen years! (They credit the original discovery to Paul Federn [1952].) They had written several articles about it, and as I read them it felt as though someone had been reading my mind. Interestingly, in the demonstration with Helen, there were probably 50 people in the room. All of them were there to learn more about hypnosis, and all of them had considerable experience in the area. However, I don't recall that a single one of them showed any sign of knowing what she was talking about in regard to Ego States.

Since then, I have talked with a few people who have found something like it, usually on their own. But very few. One thing that I hope about writing this book is that like-minded people might get together to discuss the issues. There *have* to be numbers of other clinicians out there who are stumbling upon the same thing, or possibly have been trained to work with Ego States. I hope to meet them.

Throughout this process, the question has eaten at me: if Ego States are a reality, and if there are the very large numbers of people who have them, why is there so little written about them? I don't think I really understand it. My only clue is to reflect on what I went through, and see that it was not easy at all. But I think things are a little different now than when I pursued it. There is a serial TV show depicting Multiple Personality that must be watched by millions of people. There is a comic strip in the Asheville Citizen Times called "Rose is Rose," written by Pat Brady and Don Wimmer. The main character, Rose, who is very meek and very normal, is portrayed as having an alternate personality who looks for all the world like a female biker! There are any number of references to differing personality Parts in common parlance: "That's his Alter Ego talking." "I'm of two minds on that issue." etc., etc. So the ideas of Parts and Alters have certainly made their way into the public consciousness. How many people truly believe or understand these things is another question.

When I try to teach someone to flyfish for trout, I often point out the fish in the water. Only rarely do they see the fish because the image is very subtle.

The trout's coloring blends in with the bottom of the stream, and there are only slight movements of the fins and tail to notice. Once you have seen a few hundred of them, they are easy to spot, even in fast-moving riffles. But I often forget that to the untrained eye they are virtually invisible. I think the same thing is true of both MPD and ESD. They are not usually obvious at all, and you have to have some idea of what you are looking for in order to be able to see them.

But there may also be a more personal reason that we do not see these things. Fear. It might be partly fear of the unknown and unfamiliar. And conversely, it might be fear of things that are *all too familiar*, and too close to home.

I think I experienced both kinds of fear in my own learning process. I really didn't want to see what I was seeing. It was a lot of work, it meant drastically revising my ideas about a lot of things, and I already had enough things to worry about. I don't believe any of us really want to change our ways of thinking. We resist it in many clever ways and only succumb if we have to.

When Neils Bohr discovered Quantum Theory in 1908, it irritated him. He had been working on solving a certain physics problem using the math that he had always used, but it wasn't coming out right. He worked on it for a great amount of time, and became convinced that it was only his ineptitude that was in the way. He finally resolved to present the problem at a coming physics convention so that people with keener minds than his could untie the knot. At the convention, lots of other physicists then became similarly vexed and irritated by it. In time, they began to see that there was no knot at all, but in fact the key to looking at atomic physics in a whole new way.

The second, more personal kind of fear may have something to do with seeing reflections of our own personalities in Ego State Disorder. I don't think we would find any degree of likeness to be very comforting. I'm not saying that everyone might have ESD. I don't believe that. But we all do have vicissitudes of mood and attitude and perceptual style which are unsettling to us. Life would be simpler if we were all more constant in these domains. The variability means a lot of mental work to keep up with it, and having to balance and strive for a reasonable average, or middle ground, that is workable in daily life.

But the most basic element of fear may be more like this: try to imagine waking up some morning to discover that someone has during the night shredded all our clothes, and realizing that there was no one else in the house but us. This is precisely the kind of nightmare that Multiples have to live with. In a more subtle way, I think we all fear getting out of control and having some subterranean part of ourselves take over and do great damage to our lives and our reputations. This fear, to whatever extent each of us disowns it, makes us want to put as much distance as possible between ourselves and the concept of Ego State or Alters.

One of the greatest ironies of this "discovery" process for me is that now, much later, it all seems so obvious! We all know there are *degrees* of almost everything. From the common cold to polio to depression - they all exist on a continuum. Why then did I not see immediately that the same would be true of Multiple Personality? Why would there not be some versions of it that were very serious, and some that were a great deal milder? Again, it seems so obvious now. Maybe we just learn some things very slowly.

At this point in the journey, I still have occasional doubts about ESD, but most of it feels very solid to me. I feel extremely fortunate to have gone through it. I only hope that this book will yield some useful tools in our effort to better understand these puzzling and fascinating phenomena.

Epilogue

One of the things that experimental psychologists ask of their distant relatives, clinicians, is that they provide them with testable hypotheses. In other words, when therapists make the claim that something exists, the laboratory types want them to specify how it can be proven experimentally. That seems to me a reasonable request, and I want to propose at least two methods by which I think the existence of Ego States can be tested.

First, it may be possible to administer a battery of psychological tests to different Ego States. By testing them separately, we should be able to see substantial and consistent differences among the results. These results should reflect what is known about the particular States.

This may not be easy, however. Ego States are not as enduring, rigid or constant as their counterparts, Alters. When they are "present" it is not to the same degree as with Alters. But it seems to me to be worth a try. (This procedure, by the way, has been done with Alters. The results are quite striking and clearly suggest very different psychological profiles for the various Alters.)

Another research tool that has been used with Multiples might be even more decisive for Ego States than psychological testing. Namely, the electroencephalogram, or EEG. In the experiments, one Alter is requested to come forth and perform a few simple tasks (after affixing electrodes on the person's skull). From the EEG recording, it is possible to tell which areas of the brain are most active and involved in the process. During succeeding sessions, other Alters are then called out and the same procedure is done. Although the number of studies is somewhat limited, the results indicate highly significant differences among the Alters (Pitblado, 1982 and 1986; Larmore, 1987, and Putnam, 1982).

The fact that quite different cortical patterns are noted among the various Alters is a powerful piece of evidence. It strongly suggests that the Alters are very psychologically different as well.

In September of 1992 a patient of mine requested an EEG to see if his Parts would show discernible differences. During the testing, the technician performing it said that there was little question that he was in a hypnotic state, as shown on the graph display. Two separate Ego States were elicited for about fifteen minutes each. The results unfortunately showed no significant differences in the EEG traces for the two States. However, there are several factors that need to be taken into account.

First, the EEG is a crude instrument in many ways. Prior to the experiment, I talked with one of the neuroscientists who helped in its development, and he said that it was worth a try, but he suspected that the instrument was not sensitive enough to pick up differences. He was right.

For this patient, one of the Ego States seems to reside mostly in one half of his brain. When this Part is elicited, the patient cries out of only one eye, and describes being able to feel only one half of his body. Thus, I had thought there was a chance that the EEG would pick up differences on the two sides of the brain. It did not. However, the technician explained to me afterward that we did not have the advantage of computerized averaging across time, which helps to tease out smaller differences.

Another confounding factor is that the patient had been in therapy for a good while, and there had been a fair amount of merging, or fusing, of the two States. Also, there was very little emotional involvement during the experiment, which can also account for relatively little brain activity in general. We were in a strange office with a technician that the patient had never met, and I didn't want to ask probing questions that might frighten the Parts.

I have given this account of an experimental failure because I think it is important to do so. Most professional journals are prone to report only successes, which I believe robs us of important information. This procedure will probably be attempted by others, and they should be able to do it more effectively, knowing what did not work for us.

Questionnaire

Caution: This is not a standardized test, and the results are only suggestive. A score of six or more is suggestive of Ego State Disorder, but nothing more.

1. Do you find yourself "zoning out" in the middle of a conversation, nodding your head appropriately, but having no idea what is being said?

2. Did you spend a lot of time in fantasy as a child? Did your teachers or parents say that you seemed to be "in another world" a good bit of the time?

3. Does fantasy interfere with your life as an adult? Do you escape into daydreams often as a way of dealing with uncomfortable situations?

4. Do you feel like a rather different person from time to time?

5. Do friends suggest that you seem quite changeable, different from day to day?

6. Are you accident-prone?

7. Do you make a lot of "Freudian slips" - where you think one thing, but say or write something quite different - even the opposite?

8. Do you have a sense that part of you is missing, or had to be jettisoned along the way?

9. Do you notice things about your sex life that you think are strange, like hating to be touched in ways that most people seem to enjoy?

10. Were you ever raped or molested?

11. Do you have large chunks of your childhood that are devoid of memories?

Bibliography

Csikszentmihalyi, Mihaly. <u>Flow: the Psychology of Optimal Experience.</u> New York: Harper and Row, 1990.

Federn, P. <u>Ego Psychology and the Psychoses.</u> New York: Basic Books, 1952.

Hilgard, Ernest R. <u>Divided Consciousness</u>. New York: John Wily & Sons, 1986.

Janet, P. <u>The Major Symptoms of Hysteria.</u> New York: Macmillan, 1907.

Kafka, Franz. <u>Erzahlungen,</u> 3rd ed. New York: Schocken Books, 1946.

Orne, M. T. "The simulation of Hypnosis: Why, How, and What it Means." <u>International Journal of Clinical and Experimental Hypnosis,</u> 19 (1971), pp. 183–210.

Pitblado, Colin, and Judianne Dense-Gerber. "Pattern-evoked Potential Differences among the Personalities of a Multiple: Some New Penomena." Paper presented at the 3rd annual conference on multiple personality, Chicago, IL, Sept. 18–21, 1986

Prince, M. The Dissociation of a Personality. New York: Longmans Green, 1906

Putnam, Frank W., M.D. Diagnosis and Treatment of Multiple Personality Disorder. New York: The Guilford Press, 1989.

Schiller, Friedrich. Die Rauber, Vol 3, Schillers'Werke., ed. Berbert Stubenrauch: H Bohlaus Nachfolger, 1953.

Schultz, Duane. Theories of Personality. Belmont, CA. Brooks/Cole, 1990.

Solzhenitsyn, A.I. The Gulag Archipelago., 1918–1956. New York: Harper & Row, 1973.

Waldeck, Peter B. The Split Self from Goethe to Brock. Bucknell Univ. Press, 1979.

Watkins, John, M.D. "The Bianchi Case: Sociopath or Multiple Personality?" International Journal of Clinical and Experimental Hypnosis, 32 (1984), pp. 67–101.

About the Author

Alan G. Marshall, Ph. D., is a graduate of Cornell University with a B.A. degree in Philosophy and Psychology, and he has an M.A. and a Ph.D. in Clinical Psychology, both from Vanderbilt University. His papers and publications include: "The effect of two anxiety manipulations on short-term memory." (with R. Blanton, Ph.D.), 1967; "Psychotics see themselves on Videotape", 1968, and "Depression as a pattern of emotions and Feelings", (both with C.E. Izaard, Ph.D.), New York Academic Press, 1973: and "Cerebral Electrotherapeutic Treatment of Depression", Journal of Consulting and Clinical Psychology, vol. 28 (1972).

Dr. Marshall has been married to his wife, Gail, for 47 years, and the couple have two sons - Chris and Joel. He lives in Asheville, North Carolina.